Keto Diet Instant Pot Cookbook:

Delicious and Easy Ketogenic Recipes for Your Electric Pressure Cooker to Lose Weight and Live a Healthy Life!

Karen Dixon
© February 2019

Contents

Introduction 6

Chapter 1: Keto Diet Explained 10

What is The Keto Diet? 10

Benefits of A Keto Diet 10

Dos and Don'ts of the Ketogenic Diet 13

Tips for a Successful Ketogenic Journey 15

Ketogenic Diet and Weight-Loss 18

Major Concerns about High-Fat Diets 19

Chapter 2: Basics of Using an Instant Pot 22

Benefits of Using an Instant Pot 22

Instant Pot Buttons 24

Chapter 3: Recipes 26

Soups and Stews 26

Tomato Soup 26

Rabbit Cabbage Stew 28

Beef Neck Stew 30

Hamburger Stew 32

Zucchini Soup 34

Kale Soup with Rosemary 36

Beef and Cabbage Stew 38

Chicken Curry Soup 40

Chicken and Kale Soup 42

Sichuan Pork Soup 44

Tangy Green Cabbage Stew 47

Vegan Cauliflower Soup 49

Meat (Pork, Beef, Lamb) Recipes 52

Meatloaf Recipe 52
Pork with Cauliflower 55
Tender Beef Pot Roast 58
Easy Taco Dip 60
Pork Chops with Peppers.............................. 62
Corned Beef and Cabbage.............................65
Meatloaf Cups 67
Ground Pork Taco Casserole 69
Quick & Easy Lamb Leg...............................72
Barbecue Spare Ribs 74
Ropa Vieja 76
Beef Curry 78
Tomato Pork Chops 80
Pork Saag 82
Pork Carnitas 85

Poultry Recipes 88

Chicken Liver Pâté 88
Chicken Bratwurst Meatballs with Cabbage 91
Shortcut Dan Dan–Style Chicken.................... 94
Chicken Fajitas...97
Sweet and Spicy Chicken Tinga 100
Thai Green Curry 104
Chicken Shawarma 106
Chicken Legs with Piquant Mayo Sauce.....................109
Roasted Turkey Breast Tenderloins 111
Chicken Wingettes with Cilantro Dip 113
Hot Wings 116

Turkey Breast 118
Turkey with Broccoli 120
Jalapeno Chicken 122
Turkey Stew Recipe 124

Fish and Seafood 126

Creamy Shrimp Scampi... 126
Spanish Oysters 129
Easy Lobster Bisque 131
Savory Shrimp with Tomatoes and Feta..................... 133
Tilapia Fillets with Arugula 136
Trout with Broccoli.. 138
Sour King Scallops Recipe... 141
Sweet Peppercorn Salmon 143
Baked Cod... 145
Creamy Chile Shrimp 147
Lemon Kalamata Olive Salmon.................................... 150
Seafood Medley Stew... 152
Flavored Octopus 154
Caramelized Tilapia... 156
Crunchy Almond Tuna 158

Side Dishes and Vegetables............................... 160

Veggie Scramble 160
Egg Loaf.. 162
Asparagus with Colby Cheese 164
Mexican-Style Zucchini and Poblanos 166
Vegetables à la Grecque... 169
Simple Basil Pesto Zucchini 171
Celery Spinach Stew 174

Tasty Creamy Collard Greens 177

Onion Cauliflower Hash 180

Steamed Broccoli with Basil 182

Sautéed Vegetables 184

Stuffed Bell Peppers..186

Desserts and Smoothies 189

Pumpkin Pie Pudding 189

Keto Celery and Nut Smoothie 192

Coconut-Almond Cake..194

Dark Chocolate Cake..196

Vanilla Cream with Raspberries 199

Blueberry Almond Smoothie 202

Choco-Cashew Orange Smoothie 204

Strawberry Marjoram Smoothie................................ 206

Keto Avocado Smoothie.. 208

Raspberry and Spinach Smoothie 210

Caramel Coffee Smoothie 212

Almond Choc Shake..214

Green Coconut Smoothie.. 216

Avocado Pudding 218

Conclusion.. 220
Conversion Tables 222

Introduction

I want to thank you and congratulate you for purchasing the book, *Keto Diet Instant Pot Cookbook: Delicious and Easy Ketogenic Recipes for Your Electric Pressure Cooker to Lose Weight and Live a Healthy Life.*

This book contains proven information and strategies on getting the best from the ketogenic diet using an instant pot.

With the book, you will be able to learn more about the ketogenic diet that will enrich your lifestyle. You will understand about the Instant Pot and the delicious ketogenic recipes that are made using it. Some the benefits covered in the book include:

- What is the ketogenic diet?
- Benefits of the keto diet
- Dos and Don'ts of the ketogenic diet
- Tips for a successful ketogenic journey
- Ketogenic diet and weight-loss
- Basics of using an Instant Pot … and many more!

Thanks once again for purchasing this book. Enjoy reading and embracing the keto lifestyle!

© COPYRIGHT 2019 BY KAREN DIXON

ALL RIGHTS RESERVED

In accordance with the U.S. Copyright Act of 1976, the reproduction, scanning, photocopying, recording, storing in retrieval systems, copying, transmitting, or circulating in any form by any means— electronic, mechanical, or otherwise— any part of this publication without a written permission from the publisher, constitutes piracy or theft of the author's intellectual property rights.

Exceptions only include cases of brief quotations embodied in critical reviews and/or other certain non-commercial uses permitted by copyright law. Alternatively, when using any material from this book other than reviewing simply, obtain prior permission by contacting the author, **Karen Dixon**.

ISBN: 9781797960579

Thank you for supporting the rights of the author and publisher.

NOTARIAL NOTES

The contents presented herein constitute the rights of the First Amendment. All information states to be truthful, accurate, reliable, and consistent. Any liability, by way of inattention or otherwise, to any use or abuse of any policies, processes, or directions contained within, is the sole discretion and responsibility of the recipient reader.

The presentation of the entire information is without a contract or any form of guarantees or assurances. Both author and publisher shall be, in no case, held liable for any fraud or fraudulent misrepresentations, monetary losses, damages, and liabilities—indirect or consequential—arising from event/s beyond reasonable control or relatively set out in this book.

Therefore, any information hereupon solely offers for educational purposes only, and as such, universal. It does not intend to be a diagnosis, prescription, or treatment for any diseases.

The Food and Drug Administration has not evaluated the statements in the book. If advice is necessary, consult a qualified professional for further questions concerning specific or critical matters on the subject.

The trademarks used herein are without any consent. Thus, the publication of the trademark is without any permission or backing by the trademark owner/s.
All trademarks/brands mentioned are for clarification purposes only and owned by the owners themselves not affiliated with the author or publisher.

Chapter 1: Keto Diet Explained

What is The Keto Diet?

It is a low-carb, high-fat, and moderate protein diet. The main premise behind the keto diet is to make your body more efficient at using fat for fuel instead of sugar. When you're consuming a lot of carbohydrates, your body's blood sugar levels will spike. Thus, your body will then release a hormone called insulin to help regulate your blood sugar back to normal.

Benefits of A Keto Diet

Increases HDL (Good Cholesterol)

HDL carries cholesterol away from the body towards the liver, so that it can either be excreted or reused. High levels of HDL can reduce the risk of heart disease. On a ketogenic diet, while consuming high amounts of fat, you will also ingest more "good" cholesterol.

Reduces Blood Sugar and Insulin Levels

Carbohydrates raise sugar levels in the body. Having high blood sugar is toxic and causes insulin resistance, which leads to type 2 diabetes. A reduction in carbohydrate consumption tends to lower insulin and blood sugar levels. The ketogenic diet has been proved to improve health in diabetic subjects as well as reduce or eliminate the need for insulin.

Mental Focus

Ketones provide fuel for the brain. When carbohydrate intake is decreased, it eliminates blood sugar spikes. Together, these effects can improve concentration and focus. Studies contend an increase in fatty acids can have a positive result on the overall function of the brain.

Reduces Hunger & Increases Energy

By providing your body with a more reliable source of energy, you will feel more energized throughout the day. When the body burns fats as fuel, the fats create the most energy for the body. Fat has been found to be more satisfying, so one can stay satiated for a long time period.

Epilepsy Treatment

Although the ketogenic diet has only recently gained public attention, it has been used since the 1900s as a successful treatment for epilepsy. The diet continues to be one of the most widely used therapies to treat children with uncontrollable epilepsy.

Body Weight

Weight loss is one of the major reasons why many people opt for a ketogenic diet. Research demonstrates that it fosters greater weight reduction in a much easier way. It not only helps in losing weight but also to tone our muscles and body shape.

Blood Pressure

As a ketogenic diet helps to maintain high levels of triglyceride in the body, it is also effective in controlling blood pressure and cholesterol levels. This ability, in turn, saves us from many fatal diseases, like cardiovascular diseases.

Help with Skin Problems

For people with skin problems, especially acne, this diet offers a good solution. In the absence of complex carbohydrates, there is a minimal production of toxins in the blood, so it keeps our skin healthy and acne free!

Dos and Don'ts of the Ketogenic Diet

If you are not familiar with the keto, mistakes can be made to keep you from having good health and reaping the benefits of this diet. To enhance your success with the ketogenic diet, here are some dos and don'ts:

Don't increase your carb intake
The ketogenic diet is a low-carb diet, which means you should lower your carb intake. A specific number of carbs you should have in a diet is not there. Many people follow a diet where they consume 100 to 150 grams of carbs a day. To achieve ketosis, be sure that your carbohydrate intake is low.

Most keto dieters manage the state of ketosis by consuming between 20 to 100 grams of carbs a day.

Don't fear fat
If you are on a ketogenic diet, don't be scared of fat, especially if you consume healthy fats like Omega-3s, monounsaturated fats, and saturated fats. Fats are encouraged in the ketogenic diet plan; a limit of 60 to 70% fat intake is best. To achieve these levels of fat, you must consume meat and healthy fats, such as olive oil, lard, butter, coconut, or alternatives on a daily basis.

Avoid fast food

Not having time to cook may make you turn to fast foods. However, don't even think about it. Fast foods are incredibly unhealthy and can deter you from your keto journey. Fast foods contain too many harmful chemicals and preservatives; some fast foods don't use real cheese, and their meats sometimes contain hidden sugars among other ingredients.

Increase your protein intake

Protein is an essential and important nutrient necessary for your body. It can soothe your appetite and burn fat more than any other nutrient. Generally, protein is highly effective in weight loss, can increase muscle mass, and may improve your body composition.

Increase your sodium intake

By reducing carbohydrate consumption, your insulin levels fall, which in turn gets rid of extra sodium stored in your body, causing problems such as sodium deficiency. If your body experiences sodium deficiency, you might experience exhaustion, headaches, constipations, etc.

To relieve this problem, increase your sodium intake on a keto diet. Add a teaspoon of salt to daily meals or drink a glass of water with a ¼ teaspoon of salt mixed with it.

Be patient

It is common nature for us to seek immediate gratification. When you start a diet, you may be discouraged to continue if you are not instantly experiencing the benefits immediately. Losing weight and being healthy takes time. In order to attain this goal, allow your body some time to start burning fat instead of glucose. It may take a few days or a couple of weeks, but be patient and don't bail on the diet.

Tips for a Successful Ketogenic Journey

Clear carbohydrates from your kitchen

Most people will only stick to the ketogenic diet if they have access to healthy ketogenic foods. This approach will help you in avoiding falling prey to the carbohydrate concentrated foods in your cabinet. Clean your kitchen from high-carbohydrate foods like pastry, bread, potatoes, soda, rice, and candy. This proactive approach will help a long way in achieving the ketogenic diet.

Have ketogenic snacks at hand

Having to prepare a lot of homemade meals is a big challenge for people as regards the ketogenic diet. There is a solution for you: why not have ketogenic snacks instead whenever you are hungry and you are not at home?

You can buy ketogenic snacks like hard boiled eggs, beef jerky, pre-cooked bacon, pre-made guacamole and so on, or you can have them on the go. You can prepare a lot of them, so you will not be tempted to buy carbohydrate-heavy snacks.

Buy a food scale

Although this tip might sound surprising, it is quite crucial. As it has been said, "Drops of water make an ocean." Likewise, the amount of food you eat matters even to the tiniest form. Buy a food scale to measure your food and make sure you are eating the appropriate size because even the least can make a huge difference.

For example, 2 extra tablespoons of almond butter can transform into an additional 200 calories and 6 grams of carbohydrates. However, it is not necessary you use the food scale until the end of your challenge. It is just for you to get the appropriate measurement, so then you can eyeball to measure as you continue.

Exercise frequently

I have mentioned repeatedly: exercising allows your body to break down the glycogen it has stored. It also helps you to get fit and healthy. It also helps you in maintaining your muscle mass and strengthens you.

Try intermittent fasting

This advice is one of the most effective tips that can get you right on track to achieving your fitness goals. It helps you get into ketosis and lose weight, so you do not eat anything that contains calories for a given period of time. A study in Harvard revealed that intermittent fasting manipulates your mitochondria in a way that the ketogenic diet also does to elongate your lifespan. When you stop taking calories for some time, your body will start breaking down the excess glucose in your body obtained from consuming carbohydrates.

Include coconut oil into your diet

Coconut oil contains fats called medium chain triglycerides, which enable you to quickly get into ketosis. Unlike other fats, the MCTs get quickly absorbed into the liver, where they can be used for energy or they can be converted into ketones.

Ketogenic Diet and Weight-Loss

The ketogenic diet enables the breaking down of unwanted fats and stored substances by the body. It is one of the main bodybuilding solutions to assist in lowering fat content in the body while creating muscle. Many of the bodybuilders on this regime set their everyday calorie intakes to 20% more than their typical calorie level. The figure is not rigid, but individuals adjust it accordingly to guide and adjust on an individual basis.

It is advised to load up on carbs for a three-day cycle while on the keto plan. Eat about 1000 calories of carbs on the third day a couple of hours before exercising. For carb loading, there are two options; 1) eating what you like 2) start with carbs with higher glycemic and then going to the lower ones. Carb loading is beneficial for intense workout because it enables endurance by enhancing glycogen in the muscles.

For instance, let's say you that start off carb-loading on Friday. By Sunday, your muscle tissues will have a substantial amount of glycogen in them. This day is when you ought to exercise. It is optimal to only work out half of the body at this time with weights. Schedule your next exercise routine on Wednesday and be sure to consume 1000 calories worth of carbs prior to your routine. By Wednesday, your glycogen levels will likely be low, but the pre-workout carb load will allow you to work out intensely. This time you will perform exercises targeting the other half of your body.

The next exercise session should be scheduled for Friday at the beginning of the three-day cycle of loading up on carbohydrates. This training session has to be a complete overall body workout with 1-2 sets per workout completed until failure. Make barbell rows, bench presses, military presses, barbell/dumbbell curls, triceps pushdowns, squats, lunges, deadlifts, and reverse curls the focus of your training. The goal of this exercise session is to deplete your glycogen stores within the body completely. Nevertheless, keep cardio to a minimum. Ten-minute warm-ups in advance of each workout are fine, but do not go overboard.

Major Concerns about High-Fat Diets

High protein diets are extremely seductive. After all, they can cause a massive amount of weight loss in a very short amount of time. But there is a catch because most of the weight is water.

Even worse, many additional side effects accompany high protein diets.

Therefore, here is how high protein diets can decrease your health:

Fast muscle catabolism: This process literally happens over night when you restrict carbohydrates. You see, without carbohydrates, your body turns to its own tissues for energy. In other words, you put your muscle tissue on the dinner plate.

Negative hormone production: High protein eating translates into more cortisol being released into your body. And not only does cortisol break down muscle protein, but it also lowers immunity level. Therefore, make sure you are well aware of this.

Less mental performance: Although your body can convert muscle protein to sugar for your brain, it is not a very efficient process. Subsequently, your mental performance decreases. So, if you need to maintain mental performance, high protein diets are probably not for you.

Gloomy moods: Certain neurotransmitters in your brain need carbs to replenish themselves. In turn, if you stop eating carbs, your mood will worsen. This logic is one of the main reasons why fitness professionals suffer from extreme mood swings when restricting carbs.

Less intensity: For the absolute best workouts, your body needs full levels of muscle carbohydrates. Without them, you cannot reach the potential of your intensity. Consequently, it lowers the quantity of calories your body burns outside your workouts.

Loss of definition: You need carbohydrates to achieve a toned look. In essence, carbs pull water into your muscles. If you stop eating them, your muscles dehydrate and end up looking like deflated balloons. So be conscious before avoiding carbs.

High protein diets are not all their cracked up to be. Although they do cause very rapid short-term water weight loss, they are not very good for your health.

Chapter 2: Basics of Using an Instant Pot

For so long, home cooks have been searching for a cooking method to make healthy tasty foods. Pressure cooking has become one of the hottest new culinary trends nowadays, while the Instant Pot has delivered new ideas by providing food options that are better and healthier. The Instant Pot electric pressure cooker is a multifunctional, programmable kitchen appliance that can do the job of a slow cooker, rice maker, a steamer, a sautéing pan, a warming pot, and yogurt maker.

As a modern-day pressure cooker, the Instant Pot utilizes short cooking time, high temperature, and pressure to cook food efficiently without nutrient loss. Since liquids do not evaporate in your Instant Pot, you can cook very lean meats because they remain succulent, juicy, and tender. Moreover, the Instant Pot is an eco-friendly gadget because it uses two to three times less energy than much other cookware.

Benefits of Using an Instant Pot

Cook fast and eat well. Do you think that cooking at home is time-consuming? Do all these cookware and appliances make you feel uncomfortable in the kitchen? We've got news for you – you probably don't have the right kitchen tools. The Instant Pot is an intelligent, third-generation cooker, so you don't need to stand by the stove, excessively watching and stirring your food constantly. In addition to speed, you will save your time by cooking an entire meal in the Instant Pot.

Instant Pot cooks your food as much as 70 percent quicker than other conventional cookware. You will love its hands-off functionality! Simply choose your favorite ketogenic recipe, set up the Instant Pot, sit back, relax and try to spend quality time away from the kitchen!

If you do not want to labor s all day over hot stove, the Instant Pot is the most efficient home appliance of you. The Instant Pot cooks our food way faster than conventional cookers and pots, which makes it the perfect choice for busy households.

Palatability and succulence are the main goals. High-temperature cooking produces more flavor in your meals. This cooking method requires very little fat and other flavor enhancers, so that your food retains most of their natural flavors and nutrients. Instant Pot provides a good balance of flavors because it is practically impossible to overcook the food and end up with bland food.

Health is the greatest wealth. It may sound like a cliché, but everything begins with you. Your values and health. This rationale is a logical reason why you need to cook your food properly.

Instant Pot Buttons

Sauté function is the perfect flavor-enhancing technique. You will be able to sauté your veggies before pressure cooking as well as sear and brown the meat without an additional pan.

Manual is an all-purpose button. You can adjust the time and temperature and cook almost every meal using this function.

Meat/Stew is the perfect program for cooking red meats and old-fashioned stews.

Poultry is an excellent choice for chicken, turkey, and duck.

Porridge is a function designed for cooking grains.

Rice, as the name indicates, is designed to cook all types of rice.

Soup is the fully automated function for cooking the best homemade soups and chowders quickly and effortlessly.

Bean/Chili is the program for making your favorite chilies.

Slow cook is the perfect option if you want to have a warm meal ready when you arrive home.

Multigrain is designed for cooking grains.

Yogurt is a two-step program for making homemade yogurt.

Keep Warm/Cancel is a very practical feature. Once cooking is complete, you need to push the "Cancel" button; otherwise, the warming function is automatically activated.

Chapter 3: Recipes

Soups and Stews

Tomato Soup

Serves: 4 / Prep time: 15 minutes / Cooking time: 7 minutes

Per Serving: Calories 112; Total Fat 191g; Saturated Fat 12.5g; Protein 2.7g; Total Carb 17g; Net Carb 14.9g; Fiber 2.1g; Sugar 1.5g

Ingredients:
- 2 cups tomatoes, peeled, seeded and chopped
- ½ cup vegetable broth

- ¼ teaspoon baking soda
- ¾ cup unsweetened coconut milk
- ¼ cup coconut cream
- salt and ground black pepper, as required
- 2 tablespoons fresh basil leaves, chopped

Directions:

In the pot of the Instant Pot, pour the tomatoes and broth. Secure the lid and turn to "Seal" position. Select "Manual" and cook under medium pressure for about 3 minutes.

Press the "Cancel" and allow a "Quick" release. Carefully, remove the lid and immediately, stir in baking soda until well combined.

Stir in the milk and cream. With an immersion blender, puree the soup well. Select "Sauté" and cook for about 3-4 minutes or until heated completely.

Select the "Cancel" and serve hot with the garnishing of basil.

Rabbit Cabbage Stew

Serves: 4 / Prep time: 8 minutes / Cooking time: 35 minutes

Per Serving: Calories 543; Total Fat 24.3g; Saturated Fat 13.5g; Protein 74g; Total Carb 17g; Net Carb 16.4g; Fiber 0.6g; Sugar 9.4g

Ingredients:
- 1 whole rabbit, cleaned
- 1 cup cabbage, shredded
- 4 cups beef broth
- 3 tbsp. butter

Spices:

- 1 tsp. salt
- ½ tsp. freshly ground white pepper
- 1 tsp. cayenne pepper

Directions:

Plug in your instant pot and combine all ingredients in the stainless-steel insert. Season with spices and stir until thoroughly combined. Set the steam release handle and press the "Manual" button. Set the timer for 35 minutes.

When done, perform a quick release. Optionally, transfer the goulash to a deep, heavy-bottomed pot and simmer over a medium heat until the excess liquid evaporates.

Serve warm.

Beef Neck Stew

Serves: 4 / Prep time: 15 minutes / Cooking time: 7 minutes

Per Serving: Calories 414; Total Fat 20.6g; Saturated Fat 2.5g; Protein 50.8g; Total Carb 5.4g; Net Carb 2.8g; Fiber 2.6g; Sugar 0.0g

Ingredients:
- 2 lbs. beef neck, chopped
- 2 bay leaves
- 4 tbsps. olive oil
- 3 cups beef broth
- 1 cup fire-roasted tomatoes

- 1 cup cauliflower, chopped into florets
- 1 tbsp. cayenne pepper
- 4 tbsps. Parmesan cheese
- ½ tsp. chili powder
- ½ tsp. salt

Directions:

Rinse the meat and pat dry with a kitchen paper. Place on a large cutting board and cut into bite-sized pieces and place in a large bowl. Season with salt, cayenne pepper, and chili pepper. Set aside.

Plug in the instant pot and press the "Sauté" button. Grease the bottom of the inner pot with olive oil and add the meat. Cook for 5 - 7 minutes, stirring constantly.

Now add remaining ingredients and seal the lid. Adjust the steam release handle to the "Sealing" position and press the "Meat" button. Cook for 35 minutes on high pressure.

When done, press the "Cancel" button to turn off the heat and release the pressure naturally. Make sure the pot stays covered for another 10 minutes before removing the lid.

Carefully, remove the lid and chill for a while. Divide the stew between serving bowls and sprinkle each with parmesan cheese to enjoy. Serve it immediately.

Hamburger Stew

Serves: 6 / Prep time: 10 minutes / Cook time: 7 minutes

Per serving: Calories 276; Total Fat 20.0g; Saturated Fat 7.0g; Protein 16.7g; Total Carb 8.0g; Net Carb 5.0g; Fiber 3.0g; Sugar 5.0g

Ingredients

- 1 pound 80% lean ground beef
- ½ cup tomato sauce
- 2 tablespoons tomato paste
- 1 tablespoon powdered chicken broth base
- 1 cup sliced onions
- 3 tablespoons apple cider vinegar

- 1 tablespoon soy sauce
- 1 teaspoon salt
- 2 teaspoons freshly ground black pepper
- juice of 1 lemon

Directions

Preheat the Instant Pot by selecting "Sauté" and adjusting to high heat. When the inner cooking pot is hot, add the ground beef. Break up any clumps and cook for 2 to 3 minutes. You do not need to brown the beef, as the Maillard reaction in the pressure cooker will take care of it for you.

Add the tomato sauce, tomato paste, chicken broth base, green beans, onions, vinegar, soy sauce, salt, and pepper.

Latch the lid. Select "Pressure Cook" or "Manual" and set pressure to high and cook for 5 minutes. After the time finishes, allow 10 minutes to naturally release the pressure. For any remaining pressure, just quick-release it. Open the lid.

Stir in the lemon juice and serve.

Zucchini Soup

Serves: 6 / Prep time: 15 minutes / Cooking time: 15 minutes

Per Serving: Calories 106; Total Fat 8.1g; Saturated Fat 1.3g; Protein 4.3g; Total Carbs 5.0g; Net Carb 4.0g; Fiber 1.0g; Sugar 2.2g

Ingredients:
- 3 tablespoons olive oil
- 2 medium zucchinis, chopped roughly
- 1 large leek, chopped
- 1/3 cup fresh basil, chopped and divided

- 1 tablespoon of fresh lemon juice
- sea salt, to taste
- 4 cups vegetable broth

Directions:

Add oil in the Instant Pot and select "Sauté." Now, add the zucchini and cook for about 4-5 minutes. Add leek and ¼ cup of basil and cook for about 2 minutes.

Select the "Cancel" and stir in the remaining ingredients.

Secure the lid and turn to "Seal" position. Cook on "Manual" with high pressure for about 8 minutes.

Press the "Cancel" and allow a "Natural" release. Carefully remove the lid and with an immersion blender, puree the soup.

Serve immediately with the garnishing of remaining basil.

Kale Soup with Rosemary

Serves: 4 / Prep time: 10 minutes / Cooking time: 5 minutes

Per serving: Calories 146; Total Fat 5.0g; Saturated Fat 1.0g; Protein 22.0g; Total Carb 11.5g; Net Carb 10.2g; Fiber 1.3g; Sugar 0.0g

Ingredients:
- 5 cups fresh kale, finely chopped
- 1 cup cottage cheese
- ½ tsp. minced fresh rosemary
- 1 tbsp. butter

- 3 cups vegetable broth
- ½ tsp. black pepper
- ½ tsp. pink Himalayan salt

Directions:

Rinse kale under cold running water and gently press with your hands to squeeze the liquid. Finely chopped with a sharp knife and place in the pot, along with vegetable broth, rosemary, butter, salt, and pepper.

Securely lock the lid and set the steam release handle to the "Sealing" position. Press the "Manual" button.

Set the timer for 5 minutes on high pressure.

When done, perform a quick pressure release and carefully open the lid. Stir in the cottage cheese and mix well. To enjoy, serve it immediately.

Beef and Cabbage Stew

Serves: 4 / Prep Time: 5 minutes / Cook Time: 20 minutes

Per serving: Calories 320; Total Fat 7.0g; Saturated Fat 2.0g; Protein 3.7g; Total Carb 39.1g; Net Carb 36.2g; Fiber 2.9g; Sugar 0.0g

Ingredients:
- 2 tablespoons butter
- 1 onion, chopped
- 2 garlic cloves, minced
- 1 ½ pounds beef stew meat, cubed

- 2 ½ cups beef stock
- 0.5 lb. tomato sauce, sugar-free
- 2 cups red cabbage, shredded
- 1 tablespoon coconut aminos
- 2 bay leaves
- 1 teaspoon dried parsley flakes
- 1/2 teaspoon red pepper flakes, crushed
- sea salt and ground black pepper, to taste

Directions:

Press the "Sauté" button to heat the Instant Pot. Then, melt the butter. Cook the onion and garlic until softened.

Add beef stew meat and cook an additional 3 minutes or until browned. Stir the remaining ingredients into the Instant Pot.

Secure the lid. Choose "Manual" mode and high pressure; cook for 15 minutes. Once cooking is complete, use a quick pressure release; carefully remove the lid.

Discard bay leaves and ladle into individual bowls. Enjoy!

Chicken Curry Soup

Serves: 6 / Prep Time: 10 minutes / Cook Time: 23 minutes

Per Serving: Calories 378; Total Fat 26.0g; Saturated Fat 2.0g; Protein 26.0g; Total Carbs 10.0g; Net Carbs 6.0g; Fiber 4.0g; Sugar 4.0g

Ingredients:
- 1-pound boneless, skinless chicken thighs
- 1½ cups unsweetened coconut milk
- ½ onion, finely diced
- 3 garlic cloves, crushed

- 1 cup sliced mushrooms, such as cremini and shiitake
- 0.25 lb. baby spinach
- 1 teaspoon salt
- ½ teaspoon ground turmeric
- ½ teaspoon cayenne
- 1 teaspoon garam masala
- ¼ cup chopped fresh cilantro

Directions:

In the inner cooking pot of your Instant Pot, add the chicken, coconut milk, onion, garlic, ginger, mushrooms, spinach, salt, turmeric, cayenne, garam masala, and cilantro.

Latch the lid. Select "Pressure Cook" or "Manual" and set pressure to high and cook for 10 minutes. After the time finishes, allow 5 minutes to naturally release the pressure. For any remaining pressure, just quick-release it. Open the lid.

Use tongs to transfer the chicken to a bowl. Shred the chicken and then stir it back into the soup.

Serve and enjoy!

Chicken and Kale Soup

Serves: 4 / Prep Time: 5 minutes / Cook Time: 5 minutes

Per Serving: Calories 387; Total Fat 27.0g; Saturated Fat 3.0g; Protein 26.0g; Total Carbs 10.0g; Net Carbs 8.0g; Fiber 2.0g; Sugar 2.0g

Ingredients:
- 2 cups chopped cooked chicken breast
- 0.75 lb. frozen kale
- 1 onion, chopped
- 2 cups water

- 1 tablespoon powdered chicken broth base
- ½ teaspoon ground cinnamon
- Pinch ground cloves
- 2 teaspoons minced garlic
- 1 teaspoon freshly ground black pepper
- 1 teaspoon salt
- 2 cups full-fat coconut milk

Directions:

Place the chicken, kale, onion, water, chicken broth base, cinnamon, cloves, garlic, pepper, and salt in the inner cooking pot.

Latch the lid. Select "Pressure Cook" or "Manual" and set pressure to high and cook for 5 minutes. After the time finishes, allow 10 minutes to naturally release the pressure. For any remaining pressure, just quick-release it. Open the lid.

Stir in the coconut milk. Taste and adjust any seasonings, as needed, before serving.

Sichuan Pork Soup

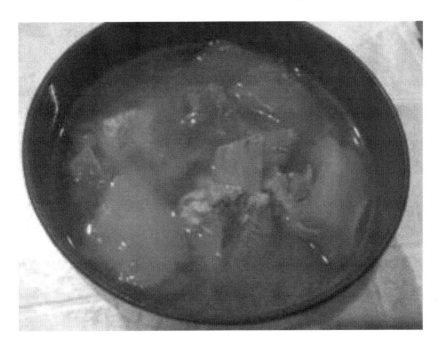

Serves: 6 / Prep Time: 10 minutes / Cook Time: 23 minutes

Per Serving: Calories 256; Total Fat 20.0g; Saturated Fat 4.0g; Protein 14.0g; Total Carbs 5.0g; Net Carb 4.0g; Fiber 1.0g; Sugar 2.0g

Ingredients:
- 2 tablespoons olive oil
- 1 tablespoon minced garlic
- 2 tablespoons soy sauce
- 2 tablespoons black vinegar

- 1 teaspoons Truvia
- 2 teaspoons Sichuan peppercorns, crushed
- 1 to 2 teaspoons salt
- ½ onion, sliced
- 1-pound pork shoulder, cut into 2-inch chunks
- 2 tablespoons doubanjiang
- 3 cups water
- 3 to 4 cups chopped bok choy
- ¼ cup chopped fresh cilantro

Directions

Select "Sauté" to preheat the Instant Pot and adjust to high heat. When the hot, add oil and let it shimmer. Add the garlic and ginger and sauté for 1 to 2 minutes.

Add the soy sauce, vinegar, sweetener, peppercorns, salt, onion, pork, doubanjiang, and water. Stir well.

Latch the lid. Select "Pressure Cook" or "Manual" and set pressure to high and cook for 20 minutes. After the time finishes, allow 10 minutes to naturally release the pressure. For any remaining pressure, just quick-release it. Open the lid.

Open the pot and add the bok choy. Close the lid and let it cook in the residual heat for about 10 minutes, or until softened, but not mushy.

Ladle the soup into bowls and top with the cilantro. Serve and enjoy!

Tangy Green Cabbage Stew

Serves: 4 / Prep Time: 3 minutes / Cook Time: 4 minutes

Per serving: Calories 114; Total Fat 8.4g; Saturated Fat 0.2g; Protein 2.8g; Total Carbs 8.1g; Net Carb 5.7g; Fiber 2.4g; Sugar 0.4g

Ingredients:
- 2 tablespoons olive oil
- ½ cup yellow onion, sliced
- 1 teaspoon garlic, smashed
- sea salt and freshly ground black pepper, to taste
- 1 teaspoon turmeric powder
- 1 serrano pepper, chopped

- 1-pound green cabbage, shredded
- 1 celery stalk, chopped
- 2 tablespoons rice wine
- 1 cup roasted vegetable broth

Directions:

Place all above ingredients in the Instant Pot.

Secure the lid. Choose "Manual" mode and high pressure; cook for 4 minutes. Once cooking is complete, use a quick pressure release; carefully remove the lid.

Divide between individual bowls and serve warm.

Vegan Cauliflower Soup

Serves: 4 / Prep Time: 7 minutes / Cook Time: 8 minutes

Per serving: Calories 144; Total Fat 11.4g; Saturated Fat 1.2g; Protein 3.3g; Total Carbs 10.0g Net Carb 9.2g; Fiber 0.8g; Sugar 3.5g

Ingredients:
- 3 teaspoons sesame oil
- 1 shallot, chopped

- 2 cloves garlic, minced
- 1 celery stalk, chopped
- ¾ pound cauliflower, broken into florets
- 4 cups water
- 4 vegan bouillon cubes
- 1 teaspoon fresh coriander, chopped
- ½ teaspoon ground cumin
- 1 teaspoon paprika
- Himalayan salt and freshly ground black pepper, to taste
- ½ cup almond milk, unsweetened
- 2 tablespoons fresh parsley, chopped

Directions

Press the "Sauté" button to heat up your Instant Pot. Heat the oil and sauté the shallot until tender or about 2 minutes. Add garlic and continue to cook for 30 seconds more, stirring frequently. Add celery, cauliflower, water, bouillon cubes, fresh coriander, cumin, paprika, salt, and black pepper.

Secure the lid. Choose "Manual" mode and low pressure; cook for 3 minutes. Once cooking is complete, use a quick pressure release; carefully remove the lid.

Then, add almond milk, press the "Sauté" button again, and let it simmer an additional 4 minutes or until everything is heated through.

Afterwards, purée the soup with an immersion blender until smooth and uniform; then, return the soup to the Instant Pot.

Ladle into soup bowls, garnish with fresh parsley, and serve warm.

Meat (Pork, Beef, Lamb) Recipes

Meatloaf Recipe

Serves: 6 / Prep Time: 20 minutes / Cook Time: 8 minutes

Per serving: Calories 358; Total Fats 18.5g; Saturated Fat 3.4g; Protein 41.4g; Total Carbs 4.0g; Net Carbs 2.3g; Fiber 1.7g; Sugar 0.1g

Ingredients:
- 2 lbs. ground pork
- 1 cup almond flour
- 2 small onions, finely chopped
- 2 spring onions, finely chopped

- ½ cup celery stalk, finely chopped
- 3 garlic cloves, crushed
- 2 tbsps. butter
- 3 tbsps. olive oil
- 1 cup cherry tomatoes, chopped.
- 2 tsps. dried celery
- ½ tsp. white pepper; ground
- 1 tsp. salt

Directions:

In a large bowl, combine the ground pork with onions, spring onions, celery stalk, and garlic. Sprinkle with salt, celery, and pepper.

Now add about one cup of almond flour and mix well again. Optionally, add a handful of finely chopped almonds for a crunchy taste.

Transfer the mixture to a large piece of plastic foil and wrap tightly. Refrigerate for 30 minutes.

Meanwhile; place cherry tomatoes in a food processor and process until smooth. Add olive oil and mix well. Set aside.

Remove the meat from the refrigerator and place back in the mixing bowl. Add tomatoes and butter. Mix well again and shape the meatloaf using a large piece of plastic foil. Place in a baking dish and loosely cover with aluminum foil.

Plug in the Instant Pot and set the trivet at the bottom of the inner pot. Pour in one cup of water and place the baking dish on top.

Seal the lid and set the steam release handle to the "Sealing" position. Press the "Manual" button and set the timer for 20 minutes on high pressure.

When done, perform a quick pressure release and open the lid. Remove the pan from the pot and chill for a while. Serve and enjoy!

Pork with Cauliflower

Serves: 6 / Prep Time: 15 minutes / Cook Time: 20 minutes

Per serving: Calories 647; Total Fats 49.2g; Saturated Fats 2.3g; Protein 45.1g; Total Carbs 3.0g; Net Carbs 1.8g; Fiber 1.2g; Sugar 0.0g

Ingredients:
- 2 lbs. pork shoulder, cut into bite-sized pieces
- 1 small onion, finely chopped
- 2 cups cauliflower, cut into florets
- 5 bacon slices, chopped.

- 2 celery stalks, chopped
- 4 tbsps. olive oil
- 4 cups beef broth
- 1 tsp. onion powder
- 2 tsps. peppercorn
- ¼ cup Stevia crystals
- ½ tsp. garlic powder
- 1 ½ tsp. salt

Directions:

Grease the bottom of the Instant Pot with oil and make the first layer with meat. Season with some salt and then add onions and celery stalks. Optionally, sprinkle with some more salt and add cauliflower. Top with bacon and gently pour in the broth.

Seal the lid and set the steam release handle to the "Sealing" position. Press the "Manual" button and set the timer for 15 minutes on high pressure.

When done, release the pressure naturally and open the lid. Remove the meat and vegetables from the pot but keep the broth.

Now press the "Sauté" button and add the stevia crystals, some more salt, peppercorn, onion powder, and garlic powder.

Gently simmer until the liquid has reduced in half.

Remove the peppercorn from the pot and add the meat. Coat well with the sauce and serve with cauliflower. Drizzle with some more sweet sauce before serving.

Tender Beef Pot Roast

Serves: 6 / Prep Time: 15 minutes / Cook Time: 50 minutes

Per serving: Calories 603; Total Fat 40.4g; Saturated Fat 2.6g; Protein 51.7g; Total Carbs 4.5g; Net Carbs 4.4g; Fiber 0.1g; Sugar 0.0g

Ingredients:
- 1 sliced onion
- 2 tbsps. minced garlic
- 2½ lbs. beef roast

- 2 tbsps. sugar-free steak sauce
- 2 chopped celery stalks
- 1 chopped bell pepper
- 2 tbsps. olive oil
- 1 cup beef broth
- 1 tbsp. balsamic vinegar
- 1½ tbsps. Italian seasoning

Directions:

Heat 1 tbsp. of olive oil in the Instant Pot on "Sauté."

Add the beef and sear it on all sides until browned: about 5 minutes in total. Transfer to a plate.

Heat the remaining oil in the Instant Pot and add the onions, celery, and pepper. Cook for a few minutes, until soft.

Add garlic and cook for 30 seconds.

Return the meat to the pot.

In a bowl, whisk together the vinegar, broth, and Italian seasoning. Pour the mixture over the beef.

Close the lid and cook on high for 40 minutes. Release the pressure naturally.

Serve and enjoy!

Easy Taco Dip

Serves: 6 / Prep Time: 5 minutes / Cook Time: 7 minutes

Per Serving: Calories 385; Total Fat 26.0g; Saturated Fat 4.1g Protein 26.0g; Total Carbs 13.0g; Net Carbs 12.0g; Fiber 1.0g; Sugar 5.0g

Ingredients:
- 1 pound 80% lean ground beef
- 1 cup chopped onion
- 4 garlic cloves, minced
- 1 (0.3 lb.) can green chiles, diced
- 1 (0.6 lb.) can tomatoes with chiles, drained

- 3 tablespoons taco seasoning
- 1½ cups grated sharp Cheddar cheese

Directions

Preheat the Instant Pot by selecting "Sauté" and adjust to high heat. When the inner cooking pot is hot, add the ground beef, onion, and garlic. Cook until the ground beef clumps have broken up, about 2 minutes.

Stir in the chiles, tomatoes, and taco seasoning.

Latch the lid. Select "Pressure Cook" or "Manual" and set pressure to high and cook for 5 minutes. After the time finishes, allow 10 minutes to naturally release the pressure. For any remaining pressure, just quick-release it. Open the lid. Add the cheese and stir until well mixed.

Pork Chops with Peppers

Serves: 5 / Prep Time: 10 minutes / Cook Time: 30 minutes

Per Serving: Calories 358; Total Fat 26.0g; Saturated Fat 4.5g; Protein 27.0g; Total Carbs 7.0g; Net Carbs 5.0g; Fiber 2.0g; Sugar 4.0g

Ingredients:
- 1 lb. pork chops, cut into bite-sized pieces
- 2 red bell peppers, sliced
- 2 bacon slices, chopped
- 2 tbsps. butter, unsalted
- 2 chili peppers, chopped

- 2 small onions, finely chopped
- 1 cup beef broth
- 2 tsp. Italian seasoning
- ¼ tsp. salt

Directions:

Rinse the meat under cold running water and sprinkle with one teaspoon of Italian seasoning. Place in the instant pot and pour in the broth.

Seal the lid and set the steam release handle. Press the "Manual" button and set the timer for 10 minutes on high pressure.

When done, release the pressure by moving the handle to the "Venting" position and carefully open the lid.

Remove the meat from the pot, along with the broth, and press the "Sauté" button.

Grease the inner pot with butter and add onion. Sauté for 2 minutes and then add peppers. Sprinkle with salt and the remaining Italian seasoning and cook for 2 - 3 minutes.

Now add bacon and stir well. Optionally, add some more salt or Italian seasoning and cook for 5 minutes. If necessary, add some beef broth – about 2 tablespoons at a time.

Finally, add the meat and give it a good stir. Cook for 5 minutes. Press the "Cancel" button and serve immediately.

Corned Beef and Cabbage

Serves: 8 / Prep Time: 5 minutes / Cook Time: 92 minutes

Per Serving: Calories 293; Total Fat 21.0g; Saturated Fat 3.9g; Protein 23.0g; Total Carbs 3.0g; Net Carbs 2.0g; Fiber 1.0g; Sugar 1.0g

Ingredients:
- 1 (3-pound) packaged corned beef brisket
- ½ head cabbage

Directions:

Add the corned beef to the inner cooking pot, fat-side up. Meat fat is a good thing.

The corned beef will come with a spice packet. Empty the spice packet into the pot. Add enough water to come up a little less than halfway to cover the meat.

Latch the lid. Select "Pressure Cook" or "Manual" and set pressure to high and cook for 90 minutes. After the time finishes, allow 10 minutes to naturally release the pressure. For any remaining pressure, just quick-release it. Open the lid.

Carefully remove the corned beef and put it on a cutting board.

Meanwhile, cut the cabbage into large chunks and put them into the water left from cooking the corned beef. Lock the lid into place. Cook on high pressure for 1 minute. When the cooking is complete, quick-release the pressure. Unlock the lid and remove the cabbage.

Slice the corned beef against the grain and serve with the cabbage.

Meatloaf Cups

Serves: 8 / Prep Time: 8 minutes / Cook Time: 25 minutes

Per serving: Calories 375; Total Fat 22.2g; Saturated Fat 4.0g; Protein 35.4g; Total Carbs 6.5g; Net Carbs 6.4g; Fiber 0.1g; Sugar 4.5g

Ingredients
- 1-pound ground pork
- 1-pound ground beef

- ½ cup onion, chopped
- 2 garlic cloves, minced
- Salt and ground black pepper, to taste
- 1/3 cup Romano cheese, grated
- ¼ cup pork rinds, crushed
- 4 eggs, whisked
- 2 ripe tomatoes, puréed
- ¼ cup barbecue sauce, sugar-free

Directions

Start by adding 1 cup of water and a metal trivet to the bottom of your Instant Pot.

In a mixing bowl, thoroughly combine ground meat, onion, garlic, salt, black pepper, cheese, pork rinds, and eggs. Mix until everything is thoroughly incorporated. Divide the mixture among muffin cups.

In a small mixing bowl, whisk puréed tomatoes with barbecue sauce. Lastly, top your muffins with the tomato sauce.

Secure the lid. Choose "Manual" mode and high pressure; cook for 25 minutes. Once cooking is complete, use a quick pressure release; carefully remove the lid.

Allow them to cool for 10 minutes before removing from the muffin tin.

Ground Pork Taco Casserole

Serves: 5 / Prep Time: 6 minutes / Cook Time: 30 minutes

Per serving: Calories 409; Total Fat 31.6g; Saturated Fat 4.2g; Protein 25.7g; Total Carbs 4.7g; Net Carbs 4.4g; Fiber 0.3g; Sugar 2.7g

Ingredients:
- 0.2 lb. cottage cheese, at room temperature
- ¼ cup double cream
- 2 eggs
- 1 teaspoon taco seasoning
- 0.4 lb. Cotija cheese, crumbled
- ¾ pound ground pork

- 1 tablespoon taco seasoning
- ½ cup tomatoes, puréed
- 0.2 lb. chopped green chilies
- 0.4 lb. Manchego cheese, shredded

Directions

Prepare your Instant Pot by adding 1 ½ cups of water and a metal rack to the bottom of the inner pot.

In a mixing bowl, thoroughly combine cottage cheese, double cream, eggs, and taco seasoning.

Lightly grease a casserole dish; spread the Cotija cheese over the bottom. Pour in the cottage egg mixture as evenly as possible.

Lower the casserole dish onto the rack.

Secure the lid. Choose "Manual" mode and high pressure; cook for 20 minutes. Once cooking is complete, use a quick pressure release; carefully remove the lid.

In the meantime, heat a cast-iron skillet over moderately high heat. Now, brown ground pork, crumbling it with a fork.

Add taco seasoning, tomato purée, and green chilies. Spread this mixture over the prepared cheese crust.

Top with shredded Manchego cheese.

Secure the lid. Choose "Manual" mode and high pressure; cook for 10 minutes. Once cooking is complete, use a quick pressure release; carefully remove the lid. Serve and enjoy!

Quick & Easy Lamb Leg

Serves: 8 / Prep Time: 7 minutes / Cook Time: 35 minutes

Per serving: Calories 432; Total Fat 25.8g; Saturated Fat 2.2g; Protein 44.7g; Total Carbs 0.9g; Net Carbs 0.6g; Fiber 0.3g; Sugar 0.0g

Ingredients:
- 1 boneless (3-4 lb.) leg of lamb
- 2 cup water
- 2 tbsp. avocado oil – divided
- 4 crushed garlic cloves
- pepper and salt, to taste
- 2 tbsp. freshly chopped rosemary

Directions

Dry the lamb using paper towels. Sprinkle with pepper and salt.

Use the "Sauté" button to start the Instant Pot, and add the oil. When hot, place the lamb in the pot and brown.

Transfer the meat to a platter and cover with the rosemary and crushed garlic.

Add the rack to the pot and arrange the lamb on it. Pour in the water and select the "Meat/Stew" setting. Cook 35 minutes. Natural release the pressure.

Preheat the oven broiler and place the lamb in a pan about six inches from the heat. Two minutes should do the trick. Let it rest about ten minutes more slicing.

Barbecue Spare Ribs

Serves: 8 / Prep Time: 5 minutes / Cook Time: 30 minutes

Per serving: Calories 444; Total Fat 33.0g; Saturated Fat 2.2g; Protein 32.5g; Total Carbs 4.4g; Net Carbs 4.2g; Fiber 0.2g; Sugar 1.7g

Ingredients:
- 3 pounds spare ribs
- sea salt and ground black pepper, to taste
- 1/2 teaspoon granulated garlic
- 1 teaspoon cayenne pepper

For the sauce:
- ¾ cup tomato puree
- a few drops of Stevia
- 1 tablespoon balsamic vinegar
- 1/3 cup broth
- 1 cup water
- 1/3 teaspoon liquid smoke
- ½ teaspoon ground cloves

Directions

Season the ribs with salt, black pepper, garlic, and cayenne pepper. Add the spare ribs to the Instant Pot.

Combine the ingredients for the sauce; whisk until everything is well mixed. Pour this sauce mixture over the spare ribs.

Secure the lid. Choose the "Meat/Stew" setting and cook for 30 minutes under high pressure. Once cooking is complete, use a natural pressure release; carefully remove the lid.

You can thicken the cooking liquid with a tablespoon or two of flaxseed meal, if desired. Enjoy!

Ropa Vieja

Serves: 4 / Prep Time: 10 minutes / Cook Time: 30 minutes

Per Serving: Calories 342; Total Fat 22.0g; Saturated Fat 3.2g Protein 24.0g; Total Carbs 12.0g; Net Carbs 9.0g; Fiber 3.0g; Sugar 6.0g

Ingredients:
- 1½ cups sliced onions
- 1 cup sliced bell peppers
- 6 garlic cloves, peeled

- 2 cups canned diced fire-roasted tomatoes, with their juices
- 1-pound beef chuck steak
- 1 teaspoon ground cumin
- 1 teaspoon salt
- 1 teaspoon smoked paprika
- ½ teaspoon ancho chili powder
- ½ teaspoon dried oregano
- ½ cup sliced pimento-stuffed olives, for garnish

Directions

Place the onions, peppers, garlic, tomatoes, steak, cumin, salt, paprika, chili powder, and oregano in the inner cooking pot.

Latch the lid. Select "Pressure Cook" or "Manual" and set pressure to high and cook for 10 minutes. After the time finishes, allow 10 minutes to naturally release the pressure. For any remaining pressure, just quick-release it. Open the lid.

Switch the Instant Pot to "Sauté" and adjust the heat to high. Bring the sauce to a boil, so it stays hot.

Meanwhile, carefully remove the steak and cut or shred it into long slices, then add it back into the sauce.

Garnish with the sliced olives and serve with a side salad or over mashed cauliflower or zucchini noodles.

Beef Curry

Serves: 4 / Prep Time: 10 minutes / Cook Time: 20 minutes

Per Serving: Calories 309; Total Fat 21.0g; Saturated Fat 2.4g; Protein 24.0g; Total Carbs 6.0g; Net Carbs 4.0g; Fiber 2.0g; Sugar 2.0g

Ingredients:
- 2 tomatoes, quartered
- 1 small onion, quartered
- 4 garlic cloves, chopped
- ½ cup fresh cilantro leaves
- 1 teaspoon ground cumin

- ½ teaspoon ground coriander
- 1 teaspoon Garam Masala
- ½ teaspoon cayenne
- 1 teaspoon salt, plus more for seasoning
- 1-pound beef chuck roast, cut into 1-inch cubes

Directions

In a blender jar, combine the tomatoes, onion, garlic, and cilantro. (If you put the tomatoes at the bottom, they will liquefy first, and you won't have to add water.)

Process until all vegetables have turned to a smooth purée. Add the cumin, coriander, garam masala, cayenne, and salt. Process for several more seconds.

Add the beef to the inner cooking pot and pour the vegetable purée on top.

Latch the lid. Select "Pressure Cook" or "Manual" and set pressure to high and cook for 20 minutes. After the time finishes, allow 10 minutes to naturally release the pressure. For any remaining pressure, just quick-release it. Open the lid.

Stir the curry. Taste and adjust, adding more salt if you like. Serve with zucchini or cucumber noodles or mashed cauliflower.

Tomato Pork Chops

Serves: 2 / Prep Time: 5 minutes / Cook Time: 9 minutes

Per Serving: Calories 274; Total Fat 19.0g; Saturated Fat 4.5g; Protein 24.0g; Total Carbs 9.0g; Net Carbs 8.0g; Fiber 1.0g; Sugar 2.0g

Ingredients:
- 2 pork chops, with bones
- 1 green bell pepper, sliced
- 1 cup cherry tomatoes
- 1 small onion, finely chopped.
- 4 tbsps. olive oil

- 1 cup beef broth
- ½ tsp. white pepper, freshly ground
- ¼ tsp. garlic powder
- ½ tsp salt

Directions

Place the meat in the pot and season with salt. Pour in the broth and seal the lid. Set the steam release handle to the "Sealing" position and press the "Manual" button.

Set the timer for 15 minutes on high pressure. When done, release the pressure naturally and open the lid.

Remove the meat from the pot and transfer to a deep bowl. Set aside

Now press the "Sauté" button and grease the inner pot with olive oil. Heat up and add onions and peppers. Sprinkle with some more salt. Cook for 5 - 6 minutes and then add cherry tomatoes. Pour in about 1/4 cup of the broth and simmer for 10 - 12 minutes, stirring occasionally.

Season with pepper and garlic powder. Optionally, add some red pepper flakes. Transfer the mixture to a food processor and process until smooth. Drizzle over pork chops and serve immediately.

Pork Saag

Serves: 4 / Prep Time: 10 minutes / Cook Time: 9 minutes

Per Serving: Calories 335; Total Fat 24.0g; Saturated Fat 3.8g; Protein 24.0g; Total Carbs 7.0g; Net Carbs 4.0g; Fiber 3.0g; Sugar 1.0g

Ingredients:
For the marinade
- ⅓ cup half-and-half, plus more as needed

- ½ teaspoon ground turmeric
- ½ teaspoon cayenne
- 2 teaspoons Garam Masala
- 1 teaspoon salt
- 1-pound pork shoulder, cut into bite-size cubes

For finishing the pork saag

- 1 tablespoon Ghee
- 1 tablespoon tomato paste
- ¾ cup water
- 0.3 lb. baby spinach, chopped
- salt, for seasoning

Directions:

To marinate the pork

In a large bowl, mix the half-and-half, garlic, ginger, turmeric, cayenne, garam masala, and salt. Add the pork and stir to coat.

Marinate the pork for at least 30 minutes or up to 8 hours. If you marinate for more than 30 minutes, cover and refrigerate the bowl until ready for use.

To finish the pork saag

Select "Sauté" to preheat the Instant Pot and adjust to high heat. When hot, add ghee and let it shimmer. Add the pork, along with the marinade, and the tomato paste. Cook for 5 to 10 minutes, or until the pork is lightly seared and the tomato paste has been well incorporated. Pour in the water.

Latch the lid. Select "Pressure Cook" or "Manual" and set pressure to high and cook for 20 minutes. After the time finishes, quick-release pressure. Open latch the lid. Select "Pressure Cook" or "Manual" and set pressure to high and cook for 2 minutes. Allow the pressure to release naturally. Unlock and remove the lid.

Mix well and adjust the seasoning, adding more salt and half-and-half, if desired.

Pork Carnitas

Serves: 4 / Prep Time: 10 minutes / Cook Time: 45 minutes

Per Serving: Calories 332; Total Fat 23.0g; Saturated Fat 3.0g; Protein 26.0g; Total Carbs 8.0g; Net Carbs 5.0g; Fiber 3.0g; Sugar 2.0g

Ingredients:
- 1 onion, sliced
- 4 garlic cloves, sliced
- 1-pound pork shoulder, cubed
- juice of 1 lemon

- ¼ teaspoon ancho chili powder
- ¼ teaspoon chipotle chili powder
- ¼ teaspoon smoked paprika
- ½ teaspoon dried oregano
- ½ teaspoon roasted cumin powder
- 1 to 2 teaspoons salt
- 1 teaspoon freshly ground black pepper
- ½ cup water
- 1 to 2 tablespoons coconut oil
- ½ cup sour cream
- ½ avocado, diced

Directions

Place the onion and garlic in the inner cooking pot to help them release water when the meat is cooking.

In a large bowl, mix together the pork and lemon juice. Add the ancho chili powder, chipotle chili powder, paprika, oregano, cumin, salt, and pepper, and stir to combine.

Place the pork on top of the onions and garlic.

Pour the water into the bowl and swirl it around to get the last of the spices. Next, pour this mixture onto the pork.

Latch the lid. Select "Pressure Cook" or "Manual" and set pressure to high and cook for 35 minutes. After the time finishes, allow 10 minutes to naturally release the pressure. For any remaining pressure, just quick-release it. Open the lid. Remove the pork, leaving the liquid in the pot.

Switch the pot to "Sauté" and adjust the heat to high to reduce the sauce while you finish the next steps.

Place a cast iron skillet on the stove over medium-high heat. Once it is hot, add the oil.

Shred the pork, then place it in a single layer in the skillet. Let the meat brown, undisturbed, for 3 to 4 minutes.

When the meat is browned on the bottom, stir it, and continue cooking until crispy in parts.

Once it's good and crisp, add in the sauce, a little at a time, from the pot. The skillet should be hot enough that most of it just evaporates, leaving behind the flavor. (I use almost all of my broth in small portions at a time, to flavor the meat.)

Serve with the sour cream and diced avocado.

Poultry Recipes

Chicken Liver Pâté

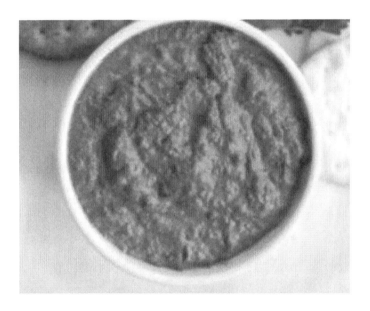

Serves: 8 / Prep Time: 5 minutes / Cook Time: 10 minutes

Per Serving: Calories 109; Total Fat 6.5g; Saturated Fat 2.2g; Protein 10.0g; Total Carbs 4.9g; Net Carbs 4.1g; Fiber 0.8g; Sugar 0.3g

Ingredients:
- 1 lb. chicken liver
- ½ cup leeks, chopped

- 2 garlic cloves, crushed
- 2 tablespoons olive oil
- 1 tablespoon poultry seasonings
- 1 teaspoon dried rosemary
- ½ teaspoon dried marjoram
- ¼ teaspoon dried dill weed
- ½ teaspoon paprika
- ½ teaspoon red pepper flakes
- salt, to taste
- ½ teaspoon ground black pepper
- 1 cup water
- 1 tablespoon stone ground mustard

Directions

Press the "Sauté" button to heat up the Instant Pot. Now, heat the oil. Once hot, sauté the chicken livers until no longer pink.

Add the remaining ingredients, except for the mustard, to your Instant Pot.

Secure the lid. Choose the "Manual" setting and cook for 10 minutes at High pressure. Once cooking is complete, use a quick pressure release; carefully remove the lid.

Transfer the cooked mixture to a food processor; add stone ground mustard. Process until smooth and uniform.

Chicken Bratwurst Meatballs with Cabbage

Serves: 4 / Prep Time: 15 minutes / Cook Time: 4 minutes

Per Serving: Calories 338; Total Fat 23.0g; Saturated Fat 1.4g; Protein 23.0g; Total Carbs 10.0g; Net Carbs 7.0g; Fiber 3.0g; Sugar 2.0g

Ingredients:
- 1-pound ground chicken
- ¼ cup heavy (whipping) cream
- 2 teaspoons salt, divided

- ½ teaspoon ground caraway seeds
- 1½ teaspoons freshly ground black pepper, divided
- ¼ teaspoon ground allspice
- 4 to 6 cups thickly chopped green cabbage
- 2 tablespoons unsalted butter

Directions

To make the meatballs, put the chicken in a bowl. Add the cream, 1 teaspoon of salt, the caraway, ½ teaspoon of pepper, and the allspice. Mix thoroughly. Refrigerate the mixture for 30 minutes. Once the mixture has cooled, it is easier to form the meatballs.

Using a small scoop, form the chicken mixture into small-to medium-size meatballs. Place half the meatballs in the inner cooking pot of your Instant Pot and cover them with half the cabbage. Place the remaining meatballs on top of the cabbage, then cover them with the rest of the cabbage.

Place pats of the butter randomly and sprinkle with the remaining 1 teaspoon of salt and 1 teaspoon of pepper.

Latch the lid. Select "Pressure Cook" or "Manual" and set pressure to high and cook for 4 minutes. After the time finishes, allow 10 minutes to naturally release the pressure. For any remaining pressure, just quick-release it. Open the lid. Serve the meatballs on top of the cabbage.

Shortcut Dan Dan–Style Chicken

Serves: 4 / Prep Time: 5 minutes / Cook Time: 7 minutes

Per Serving: Calories 297; Total Fat 17.0g; Saturated Fat 0.9g; Protein 26.0g; Total Carbs 10.0g; Net Carbs 5.0g; Fiber 5.0g; Sugar 3.0g

Ingredients:
- 2 tablespoons olive oil
- 1 tablespoon doubanjiang
- 2 teaspoons soy sauce

- 2 teaspoons rice wine vinegar
- ½ to 2 teaspoons red pepper flakes
- 1 teaspoon ground Sichuan peppercorns
- ¼ cup hot water
- 1-pound boneless, skinless chicken breast, cut into bite-size pieces
- ¼ cup room-temperature water
- 1 (½ pound) package shirataki noodles, rinsed
- 1 tablespoon sesame oil
- ¼ cup chopped fresh cilantro (optional)

Directions

In a medium bowl, mix together the olive oil, doubanjiang, soy sauce, vinegar, red pepper flakes, peppercorns, and hot water.

Put the chicken in the bowl and mix, so the chicken is well coated. For the best results, let the chicken marinate for 30 minutes.

Put the chicken and marinade in the inner cooking pot. Pour in the room-temperature water.

Latch the lid. Select "Pressure Cook" or "Manual" and set pressure to high and cook for 7 minutes. After the time finishes, allow 10 minutes to naturally release the pressure. For any remaining pressure, just quick-release it. Open the lid. While the chicken is cooking, prepare the shirataki noodles according to the package instructions.

Mix the chicken with the noodles. Just before serving, stir in the sesame oil. Serve garnished with the peanuts and cilantro (if using).

Chicken Fajitas

Serves: 4 / Prep Time: 20 minutes / Cook Time: 10 minutes

Per Serving: Calories 322; Total Fat 6.1g; Saturated Fat 1.1g; Protein 50.4g; Total Carbs 11.5g; Net Carbs 11.1g; Fiber 0.4g; Sugar 0.2g

Ingredients:
- 1 lb. chicken breast, chopped into bite-sized pieces
- 1 onion, finely chopped
- 1 tbsp lime juice
- 6 large leaves Iceberg lettuce
- 2 tbsps. homemade taco seasoning

- 1 cup cherry tomatoes, chopped
- 3 garlic cloves, minced
- 1 bell pepper, cut into strips

Taco seasoning:
- 1 tbsp. smoked paprika
- ½ tsp. coriander powder
- ½ tsp. black pepper, freshly ground
- 3 tbsps. chili powder
- 1 tsp onion powder
- 2 tbsps. pink Himalayan salt
- 2 tsps. garlic powder
- 2 tsps. oregano

Directions

Combine all ingredients for taco seasoning in a jar and shake well. Set aside.

Rinse the meat well and place in a deep bowl. Generously sprinkle with taco seasoning. Place in the pot and add tomatoes, garlic, sliced peppers, onions, and lime juice

Seal the lid and press the "Poultry" button. Set the timer for 8 minutes on high pressure.

When done, perform a quick release and open the lid. Remove the mixture from the pot and place in a bowl. Cool completely.

Spread about 2 - 3 tablespoons of the mixture at the center of each lettuce leaf and wrap tightly. Secure each wrap with a toothpick and serve immediately.

Cut the chicken into bite-size pieces. Add it back to the sauce.

Preheat the Instant Pot by selecting "Sauté" and adjust to less for low heat. Let the chicken heat through. Break it up into smaller pieces if you like, but don't shred it.

Serve over cauliflower rice or raw cucumber noodles.

Sweet and Spicy Chicken Tinga

Serves: 6 / Prep Time: 10 minutes / Cook Time: 30 minutes

Per Serving: Calories 260; Total Fat 16.0g; Saturated Fat 0.2g; Protein 24.0g; Total Carbs 9.0g; Net Carbs 6.0g; Fiber 3.0g; Sugar 4.0g

Ingredients:
- 4 teaspoons vegetable oil
- 2 tomatillos, cut into thin slices
- ½ onion, cut into thin slices
- 3 garlic cloves
- 1 (0.9 lb.) can fire-roasted tomatoes
- ⅓ cup chicken broth

- 1 chipotle chile with adobo sauce from a can, chopped
- ½ teaspoon ground cumin
- ¼ teaspoon ground cinnamon
- ½ teaspoon dried oregano
- 1 teaspoon Truvia or Swerve
- 1 tablespoon fish sauce or soy sauce
- 1 tablespoon cider vinegar
- 1½ pounds boneless, skinless chicken thighs
- ½ cup sour cream
- 2 teaspoons lemon juice
- 1 avocado, sliced

Directions

Select "Sauté" to preheat the Instant Pot and adjust to high heat. When the hot, add oil and let it shimmer.

Add the tomatillo slices in a single layer and then add the onions as a flat layer between the tomatillo slices. Nestle in the garlic cloves. You're going to let them char, so do not stir them.

Once the thinner slices start to look a little burned, flip the vegetables. The bottom of the pot will have large black spots where the vegetables have charred, but this is a good sign.

Once the vegetables are well charred, add the tomatoes and broth and deglaze the pan, scraping up all the lovely brown bits from the bottom. Do this really well and ensure there are no burned bits remaining on the bottom. Otherwise, your Instant Pot will not come to pressure.

Add the chipotle, cumin, cinnamon, oregano, sweetener, fish sauce, and vinegar. Cook for 1 to 2 minutes to allow the spices to bloom. Add the chicken.

Latch the lid. Select "Pressure Cook" or "Manual" and set pressure to high and cook for 15 minutes. After the time finishes, allow 10 minutes to naturally release the pressure. For any remaining pressure, just quick-release it. Open the lid.

Remove the chicken and shred it.

Tilting the pot, use an immersion blender to purée the sauce until the mixture is smooth.

Turn the pot to "Sauté" and adjust to high heat; then cook to thicken the sauce for about 10 minutes. Once it's thickened a bit, add in the chicken and heat.

While the chicken heats, make a crema in a small bowl by mixing together the sour cream and lemon juice.

Top the chicken with the crema and avocado slices. Serve over cauliflower rice or wrapped in lettuce leaves for a low-carb option. You can also use low-carb corn tortillas.

Thai Green Curry

Serves: 6 / Prep Time: 10 minutes / Cook Time: 8 hours

Per Serving: Calories 290; Total Fat 20.0g; Saturated Fat 0.0g; Protein 17.0g; Total Carbs 12.0g; Net Carbs 9.0g; Fiber 3.0g; Sugar 0.0g

Ingredients:
- 1 tablespoon coconut oil
- 2 tablespoons Thai green curry paste (adjust to your preferred spice level)
- 1 tablespoon minced fresh ginger
- 1 tablespoon minced garlic
- ½ cup sliced onion
- 1-pound boneless, skinless chicken thighs

- 2 cups peeled, chopped eggplant
- 1 cup chopped green, yellow, or orange bell pepper
- ½ cup fresh basil leaves, preferably Thai basil
- 1½ cups unsweetened coconut milk
- 1 tablespoon fish sauce
- 2 tablespoons soy sauce
- 2 teaspoons Truvia or Swerve
- salt, to taste

Directions

Select "Sauté" to preheat the Instant Pot and adjust to high heat. When the hot, add coconut oil and let it shimmer. Add the curry paste and cook for 1 to 2 minutes, stirring occasionally.

Add the ginger and garlic and stir-fry for 30 seconds. Add the onion and stir it all together.

Add the chicken, eggplant, bell pepper, basil, coconut milk, fish sauce, soy sauce, and Truvia or Swerve. Stir to combine.

Press "Cancel" to turn off "Sauté" mode, and switch to "Slow Cook" mode. Adjust to cook for 8 hours on medium (not low).

When the curry has finished cooking, add salt to taste.

Chicken Shawarma

Serves: 4 / Prep Time: 10 minutes / Cook Time: 15 minutes

Per Serving: Calories 267; Total Fat 15.0g; Saturated Fat 2.1g; Protein 28.0g; Total Carbs 5.0g; Net Carbs 4.0g; Fiber 1.0g; Sugar 4.0g

Ingredients:
- 1-pound boneless, skinless chicken thighs or breasts, cut into large bite-size chunks
- 3 teaspoons extra-virgin olive oil, divided
- 3 tablespoons Shawarma Spice Mix

- 1 cup thinly sliced onions
- ¼ cup water
- 4 large lettuce leaves
- 1 cup Tzatziki Sauce

Directions

Place the chicken in a zip-top bag and add 1 teaspoon of olive oil and the shawarma spice mix. Mash it all together, so that the chicken is evenly coated in the oil and spices.

At this point, you can freeze the chicken for a meal later in the week, or you could leave it in the refrigerator to marinate for up to 24 hours. (I like to make half the chicken now and freeze the other half for another meal. Clearly this "now and later" is a thing with me.)

Select "Sauté" to preheat the Instant Pot and adjust to high heat. When the hot, add the remaining 2 teaspoons of oil and let it shimmer. Add the chicken in a single layer. Let it sear, then flip the pieces to the other side, about 4 minutes in total.

Add the onion.

Pour in the water and scrape up any browned bits from the bottom of the pot.

Latch the lid. Select "Pressure Cook" or "Manual" and set pressure to high and cook for 10 minutes. After the time finishes, allow 10 minutes to naturally release the pressure. For any remaining pressure, just quick-release it. Open the lid. To serve, wrap the chicken in the lettuce leaves and serve with the tzatziki sauce.

Chicken Legs with Piquant Mayo Sauce

Serves: 4 / Prep Time: 6 minutes / Cook Time: 19 minutes

Per Serving: Calories 484; Total Fat 42.6; Saturated Fat 0.5g; Protein 22.3g; Total Carbs 2.4g; Net Carbs 2.1g; Fiber 0.3g; Sugar 5.0g

Ingredients:
- 4 chicken legs, bone-in, skinless
- 2 garlic cloves, peeled and halved
- ½ teaspoon coarse sea salt
- ¼ teaspoon ground black pepper, or more to taste
- ½ teaspoon red pepper flakes, crushed

- 1 tablespoon olive oil
- ¼ cup chicken broth

Dipping Sauce:
- ¾ cup mayonnaise
- 2 tablespoons stone ground mustard
- 1 teaspoon fresh lemon juice
- ½ teaspoon Sriracha

Topping:
- ¼cup fresh cilantro, roughly chopped

Directions

Rub the chicken legs with garlic halves; then, season with salt, black pepper, and red pepper flakes. Press the "Sauté" button.

Once hot, heat the oil and sauté chicken legs for 4 to 5 minutes, turning once during cooking time. Add a splash of chicken broth to deglaze the bottom of the pan.

Secure the lid. Choose "Manual" mode and high pressure; cook for 14 minutes. Once cooking is complete, use a natural pressure release; carefully remove the lid.

Meanwhile, mix all ingredients for the dipping sauce; place in the refrigerator until ready to serve.

Garnish chicken legs with cilantro. Serve with the piquant mayo sauce on the side.

Roasted Turkey Breast Tenderloins

Serves: 6 / Prep Time: 6 minutes / Cook Time: 34 minutes

Per Serving: Calories 255; Total Fat 7.1g; Saturated Fat 0.0g; Protein 49.7g; Total Carbs 0.7g; Net Carbs 0.4g; Fiber 0.3g; Sugar 0.0g

Ingredients:
- 6 turkey breast tenderloins
- 4 cloves garlic, halved
- 2 tablespoons grapeseed oil
- ½ teaspoon paprika

- ½ teaspoon dried basil
- ½ teaspoon dried oregano
- ½ teaspoon dried marjoram
- 1 cup water
- sea salt, to taste
- ¼ teaspoon ground black pepper

Directions

Rub turkey fillets with garlic halves. Now, massage 1 tablespoon of oil into your turkey and season it with paprika, basil, oregano, marjoram, water, salt, and black pepper. Press the "Sauté" button and add another tablespoon of oil. Brown the turkey fillets for 3 to 4 minutes per side.

Add the rack to the Instant Pot; lower the turkey onto the rack.

Secure the lid. Choose the "Manual" setting and cook for 30 minutes. Once cooking is complete, use a natural pressure release; carefully remove the lid.

Serve right away.

Chicken Wingettes with Cilantro Dip

Serves: 6 / Prep Time: 60 minutes / Cook Time: 6 minutes

Per Serving: Calories 296; Total Fat 22.5g; Saturated Fat 1.2g; Protein 10.8g; Total Carbs 11.3g; Net Carbs 10.8g; Fiber 0.5g; Sugar 1.0g

Ingredients:
- 10 fresh cayenne peppers, trimmed and chopped
- 3 garlic cloves, minced
- 1 ½ cups white vinegar

- ½ teaspoon black pepper
- 1 teaspoon sea salt
- 1 teaspoon onion powder
- 12 chicken wingettes
- 2 tablespoons olive oil

Dipping Sauce:
- ½ cup mayonnaise
- ½ cup sour cream
- ½ cup cilantro, chopped
- 2 cloves garlic, minced
- 1 teaspoon smoked paprika

Directions

Place cayenne peppers, 3 garlic cloves, white vinegar, black pepper, salt, and onion powder in a container. Add chicken wingettes, and let them marinate, covered, for 1 hour in the refrigerator.

Add the chicken wingettes, along with the marinade and olive oil to the Instant Pot.

Secure the lid. Choose the "Manual" setting and cook for 6 minutes. Once cooking is complete, use a quick pressure release; carefully remove the lid.

In a mixing bowl, thoroughly combine mayonnaise, sour cream, cilantro, garlic, and smoked paprika.

Serve warm chicken with the dipping sauce on the side.

Hot Wings

Serves: 8 / Prep Time: 15 minutes / Cook Time: 15 minutes

Per Serving Calories 334; Total Fat 26.0g; Saturated Fat 2.0g; Protein 22.0g; Total Carbs 4.0g; Net Carbs 3.0g; Fiber 1.0g; Sugar 0.5g

Ingredients:
- 1 cup hot sauce (ex. Frank's Red Hot)
- 3 tbsps. lime juice
- 3 minced garlic cloves

- pepper and salt, to taste
- 1 tbsp. avocado oil – optional
- 2 lbs. chicken wings

Ranch Dip Ingredients

- ½ cup chopped flat leaf parsley
- 1 cup sour cream
- 3 freshly chopped chives
- 1 tsp. sea salt
- 1 tsp. ground black pepper
- ½ tsp. cayenne pepper

Directions

Sprinkle the wings with the salt and pepper. Empty the sauce into a bowl, along with the chicken. Marinate overnight or at least two hours.

When ready to prepare, dump the chicken and marinade along with the rest of the fixings (omit the ranch). Close the lid and use the "Manual" setting for five minutes. Natural release the pressure ten minutes and quick release to open after that time.

Prepare the ranch dip and chill.

Turkey Breast

Serves: 2 / Prep Time: 4 minutes / Cook Time: 8 minutes

Per Serving: Calories 268; Total Fat 10.7g; Saturated Fat 0.7g; Protein 29.9g; Total Carbs 9.0g; Net Carbs 8.8g; Fiber 0.2g; Sugar 1.0g

Ingredients:
- 2 turkey breast fillets
- 1 cup water
- 1 tbsp. rosemary
- 1 tbsp. garlic powder

- 1 tbsp. sage
- ¼ tsp. pepper
- ½ tsp. salt
- ½ tsp. thyme

Directions

Arrange the rack in the Instant Pot or just add the breast to the water for poaching.

Use the spices and herbs to rub the turkey and place them into the pot. Secure the lid using the "Poultry" function (7-10 min).

Quick release the pressure when the time is done and remove the meat.

You can use the juices with the meat or save it for a broth later.

Turkey with Broccoli

Serves: 3 / Prep Time: 15 minutes / Cook Time: 35 minutes

Per Serving: Calories 327; Total Fat 24.5g; Saturated Fat 1.0g; Protein 29.8g; Total Carbs 1.5g; Net Carbs 1.3g; Fiber 0.2g; Sugar 0.4g

Ingredients:
- ½ pound ground turkey
- 1 spring onion, finely chopped
- 1 cup broccoli, chopped
- 1 cup shredded mozzarella
- 3 tbsps. sour cream

- ¼ cup Parmesan cheese, grated
- 2 tbsps. olive oil
- ¼ cup chicken stock
- ¼ tsp. dried oregano
- ¼ tsp. white pepper, freshly ground
- ½ tsp. dried thyme
- ½ tsp. salt

Directions

Plug in the Instant Pot and press the "Sauté" button. Add olive oil and heat up.

Now add spring onions and cook for 1 minute, stirring constantly.

Add turkey and broccoli. Pour in the stock and cook for 12 - 15 minutes, stirring occasionally. Season with salt, pepper, thyme, and oregano and stir in the cheese.

Press the "Cancel" button and remove from the pot. Transfer the mixture to a small baking dish and set aside.

Preheat the oven to 350° F and bake for 15 - 20 minutes, or until lightly charred.

Remove from the oven and chill for a while. Top with sour cream and serve.

Jalapeno Chicken

Serves: 4 / Prep Time: 15 minutes / Cook Time: 15 minutes

Per Serving: Calories 358; Total Fat 11.9g; Saturated Fat 1.0g; Protein 55.0g; Total Carbs 4.5g; Net Carbs 3.1g; Fiber 1.4g; Sugar 0.0g

Ingredients:
- 5 chicken thighs, skin on
- 1 large onion, chopped
- 3 jalapeno peppers, chopped

- ¾ cup cauliflower, chopped into florets
- 1 chili pepper, chopped
- 3 tbsps. fish sauce
- 1 tbsps. Swerve
- 5 cups chicken stock
- 2 tbsps. extra virgin olive oil
- 3 bay leaves
- 1 tsp peppercorn
- 1 tsp dried thyme
- 1½ tsp salt

Directions

Combine all ingredients in the instant pot and stir well. Seal the lid and set the steam release handle to the "Sealing" position.

Press the "Poultry" button and set the timer for 20 minutes on high heat.

When done, release the pressure naturally and open the lid. Remove the meat from the bones and stir well again. Serve with some grated Parmesan cheese.

Turkey Stew Recipe

Serves: 5 / Prep Time: 10 minutes / Cook Time: 20 minutes

Per Serving: Calories 386; Total Fat 20.1g; Saturated Fat 2.0g; Protein 36.2g; Total Carbs 12.0g; Net Carbs 11.3g; Fiber 0.7g; Sugar 0.0g

Ingredients:
- 2 lbs turkey breast, chopped into smaller pieces
- 2 cups cherry tomatoes, chopped
- 1 onion, finely chopped
- 4 cups chicken broth

- ¾ cup heavy cream
- 2 celery stalks, chopped
- 4 tbsps. butter
- 1 tsp. dried thyme
- 1 tsp. peppercorn
- 2 tsps. salt

Directions

Combine the ingredients in the instant pot and seal the lid

Set the steam release handle to the "Sealing" position and press the "Stew" button. Set the timer for 20 minutes on high heat.

When done; release the pressure naturally and open the lid. Chill for a while and stir in some sour cream. To enjoy, serve it immediately.

Fish and Seafood

Creamy Shrimp Scampi

Serves: 6 / Prep Time: 5 minutes / Cook Time: 4 minutes

Per Serving: Calories 332; Total Fat 23.0g; Saturated Fat 0.4g; Protein 28.0g; Total Carbs 4.0g; Net Carbs 4.0g; Fiber 0.0g; Sugar 0.0g

Ingredients:
- 2 tablespoons unsalted butter
- 4 garlic cloves, minced

- ¼ teaspoon red pepper flakes, or to taste
- ½ teaspoon smoked paprika
- 1-pound frozen peeled shrimp
- ½ to 1 teaspoon salt
- 1 teaspoon freshly ground black pepper
- ½ cup water or chicken broth
- ½ cup heavy (whipping) cream
- ½ cup Parmesan cheese
- 2 cups cooked zucchini noodles

Directions

Preheat the Instant Pot by selecting "Sauté" and adjust to high heat. When the inner cooking pot is hot, add the butter and heat until it foams. Add the garlic and red pepper flakes; then sauté until the garlic is slightly browned, 1 to 2 minutes.

Add the paprika and then the frozen shrimp, salt, and pepper.

Pour in the water or broth. If using water, add ½ teaspoon of salt.

Latch the lid. Select "Pressure Cook" or "Manual" and set pressure to high and cook for 2 minutes. After the time finishes, allow 10 minutes to naturally release the pressure. For any remaining pressure, just quick-release it. Open the lid. Turn the pot to "Sauté" and adjust to high heat. Add the cream and cheese, and stir until melted and combined, about 1 minute.

Portion the zucchini noodles in individual bowls or plates, and then top each one with the creamy shrimp scampi. Serve immediately.

Spanish Oysters

Serves: 6 / Prep Time: 8 minutes / Cook Time: 8 minutes

Per Serving: Calories 185; Total Fat 10.0g; Saturated Fat 0.0g; Protein 24.0g; Total Carbs 2.0g; Net Carbs 2.0g; Fiber 0.0g; Sugar 0.0g

Ingredients:
- 18 oysters, scrubbed clean
- ¼ cup cilantro, chopped
- 2 tomatoes, chopped
- 1 jalapeno pepper, chopped
- ¼ cup red onion, finely chopped

- salt and black pepper, to taste
- ½ cup Monterey Jack cheese, shredded
- juice from 1 lime
- 2 limes, cut into wedges

Directions

In a bowl, mix together onion, jalapeno, cilantro, tomatoes, salt, pepper, lime juice, and stir well.

Place oysters on a preheated grill over medium high heat, cover, and cook for 7 minutes until the oysters open.

Transfer opened oysters to a baking dish, and discard unopened ones.

Top oysters with cheese and place under a preheated broiler for 1 minute.

Arrange oysters on a platter and top each with the salsa mix made earlier. Finally, serve with lime wedges on the side.

Easy Lobster Bisque

Serves: 4 / Prep Time: 10 minutes / Cook Time: 8 minutes

Per Serving: Calories 441; Total Fat 30.0g; Saturated Fat 0.0g; Protein 30.0g; Total Carbs 14.0g; Net Carbs 10.0g; Fiber 4.0g; Sugar 5.0g

Ingredients:
- 2 teaspoons Ghee or unsalted butter
- 1 onion, chopped
- 1 tablespoon minced garlic
- 1 tablespoon minced fresh ginger
- 2 cups chicken broth

- 1 cup chopped tomatoes
- 3 cups chopped cauliflower
- 2 tablespoons ready-made pesto
- ½ teaspoon salt
- 1 teaspoon freshly ground black pepper
- 1-pound cooked lobster meat
- 1 cup heavy (whipping) cream

Directions

Select "Sauté" to preheat the Instant Pot and adjust to high heat. When hot, add the ghee and allow it to shimmer. Add the onion, garlic, and ginger. Sauté until softened, 2 to 3 minutes.

Pour in the chicken broth and stir, scraping the bottom of the pan to loosen any browned bits. Add the tomatoes, cauliflower, pesto, salt, and pepper.

Latch the lid. Select "Pressure Cook" or "Manual" and set pressure to high and cook for 4 minutes. After the time finishes, allow 10 minutes to naturally release the pressure. For any remaining pressure, just quick-release it. Open the lid. Tilting the pot, use an immersion blender to purée the vegetables into a smooth soup.

Turn the pot to "Sauté" and adjust to high heat. Add the lobster meat and cook until it is heated through. Stir in the cream and serve.

Savory Shrimp with Tomatoes and Feta

Serves: 6 / Prep Time: 10 minutes / Cook Time: 2 minutes

Per Serving: Calories 361; Total Fat 22.0g; Saturated Fat 0.2g; Protein 30.0g; Total Carbs 13.0g; Net Carbs 11.0g; Fiber 2.0g; Sugar 2.0g

Ingredients:

- 3 tablespoons unsalted butter

- 1 tablespoon garlic
- ½ teaspoon red pepper flakes, or more as needed
- 1½ cups chopped onion
- 1 (0.9 lb.) can diced tomatoes, undrained
- 1 teaspoon dried oregano
- 1 teaspoon salt
- 1-pound frozen shrimp, peeled
- 1 cup crumbled feta cheese
- ½ cup sliced black olives
- ¼ cup chopped parsley

Directions

Preheat the Instant Pot by selecting "Sauté" and adjusting to high heat. When the inner cooking pot is hot, add the butter and heat until it foams. Add the garlic and red pepper flakes and cook just until fragrant, about 1 minute.

Add the onion, tomatoes, oregano, and salt, and stir to combine. Add the frozen shrimp.

Latch the lid. Select "Pressure Cook" or "Manual" and set pressure to high and cook for 20 minutes. After the time finishes, quick-release it. Open the lid. Mix the shrimp in with the lovely tomato broth.

Allow the mixture to cool slightly. Right before serving, sprinkle with the feta cheese, olives, and parsley. This dish makes a soupy broth, so it's great over mashed cauliflower.

Tilapia Fillets with Arugula

Serves: 4 / Prep Time: 5 minutes / Cook Time: 5 minutes

Per Serving: Calories 145; Total Fat 4.9g; Saturated Fat 0.0g; Protein 23.3g; Total Carbs 2.4g; Net Carbs 2.0g; Fiber 0.4g; Sugar 0.0g

Ingredients:
- 1 lemon, juiced
- 1-pound tilapia fillets
- 2 teaspoons ghee
- sea salt and ground black pepper, to taste

- ½ teaspoon cayenne pepper, or more to taste
- ½ teaspoon dried basil
- 2 cups arugula

Directions

Add fresh lemon juice and 1 cup of water to the bottom of your Instant Pot. Add a metal steamer insert.

Brush the fish fillets with melted ghee.

Season the fish with salt, black pepper, cayenne pepper; arrange the tilapia fillets in the steamer insert; sprinkle dried basil on top of the fish.

Secure the lid. Choose "Manual" mode and low pressure; cook for 4 minutes. Once cooking is complete, use a quick pressure release; carefully remove the lid.

Serve with fresh arugula and enjoy!

Trout with Broccoli

Serves: 5 / Prep Time: 10 minutes / Cook Time: 25 minutes

Per Serving: Calories 488; Total Fat 27.2g; Saturated Fat 0.0g; Protein 54.2g; Total Carbs 3.3g; Net Carbs 1.6g; Fiber 1.7g; Sugar 0.0g

Ingredients:
- 2 lbs. trout fillets, skin-on
- 2 tbsps. butter
- 2 tbsps. apple cider vinegar
- 4 cups fish stock
- 3 cups broccoli, chopped

- 1 small onion, finely chopped
- ¼ cup olive oil
- ½ tsp. chili flakes
- ¼ tsp. garlic powder
- ½ tsp. dried celery
- 1 tsp. chili powder
- ½ tsp. salt

Directions:

Remove the fish from the refrigerator about an hour before using. Rub with olive oil and sprinkle with salt, dried celery, chili powder, chili flakes, and garlic powder. Place in a deep bowl and cover with a lid. Set aside.

Plug in the Instant Pot and pour in the fish stock. Add broccoli and stir well. Seal the lid and set the steam release handle to the "Sealing" position. Set the timer for 20 minutes.

When done, perform a quick pressure release and open the lid. Remove the cauliflower from the pot and drain. Place in a deep bowl and mash with a potato masher. Optionally, transfer to a food processor and process until smooth. Set aside.

Place the steam insert in the pot and place the fish in it. Pour in 2 cups of water and seal the lid. Set the steam release handle again and press the "Fish" button.

When done; perform a quick pressure release and open the lid. Remove the fish from the pot and press the "Sauté" button.

Add mashed broccoli and stir in the butter. Optionally, sprinkle with some salt and garlic powder. Heat up and remove from the pot. Serve with steamed fish.

Sour King Scallops Recipe

Serves: 4 / Prep Time: 15 minutes / Cook Time: 15 minutes

Per Serving: Calories 389; Total Fat 31.3g; Saturated Fat 0.3g; Protein 27.1g; Total Carbs 31.3g; Net Carbs 31.3g; Fiber 0.0g; Sugar 0.0g

Ingredients:
- 5 king scallops, fresh
- 2 tbsps. olive oil
- 3 tbsps. butter
- 1 tbsp. fresh lemon juice
- 1 medium-sized onion, finely chopped
- ¼ cup apple cider vinegar

- 1 cup fish stock
- ½ tsp. garlic powder
- ½ tsp. white pepper, freshly ground
- 1 tsp. salt

Directions

Plug in the Instant Pot and grease the inner pot with olive oil. Heat up and add onions. Cook for 3 - 4 minutes, or until translucent.

Pour in the stock and apple cider vinegar. Add scallops and gently simmer for 5 minutes.

Season with salt, garlic powder, and white pepper. Give it a good stir and press the "Cancel" button.

Seal the lid and set the steam release handle. Press the "Manual" button and set the timer for 8 minutes.

When done, perform a quick pressure release and open the lid.

Stir in the butter and sprinkle with lemon juice. Serve it and enjoy immediately!

Sweet Peppercorn Salmon

Serves: 4 / Prep Time: 5 minutes / Cook Time: 15 minutes

Per Serving: Calories 395; Total Fat 28.0g; Saturated Fat 0.0g; Protein 32.0g; Total Carbs 4.0g; Net Carbs 3.7g; Fiber 0.3g; Sugar 0.0g

Ingredients:
- 4 (600 g.) salmon fillets
- 1 tsp. black pepper, coarsely ground
- 2 tbsps. parsley

- ½ tsp. minced ginger
- 1 tbsp. lemon juice
- salt, to taste
- 1 pinch Stevia concentrate (optional)
- 1 tbsp. apple cider vinegar
- ½ cup heavy cream
- 3 tbsps. butter

Directions

Select the "Sauté" option on the Instant Pot and add butter, ginger, stevia, lemon juice, and vinegar. Cook for about a minute.

Rub the salmon fillets with salt and pepper and place inside the Instant Pot. Spoon sauce over the fillets. Add ¼ cup water and cook on low pressure for 1 minute.

Release pressure manually. Flip with care and sauté salmon until cooked to your liking. Remove salmon from the pot and let the sauce simmer for an additional 3 to 4 minutes. Add heavy cream and stir until well combined.

Drizzle sauce over the fillets and garnish with parsley.

Baked Cod

Serves: 3 / Prep Time: 2 minutes / Cook Time: 5 minutes

Per Serving: Calories 395; Total Fat 28.0g; Saturated Fat 0.0g; Protein 29.0g; Total Carbs 9.0g; Net Carbs 9.0g; Fiber 0.0g; Sugar 0.0g

Ingredients:
- 0.125 lbs. cherry tomatoes
- pinch of salt and pepper
- 1 tbsp. chili seasoning mix
- 0.25 lb. raw avocado

- 1lb. atlantic cod fillet, sliced into pieces
- 2 tbsps. melted coconut oil
- 1 tbsp. olive oil

Directions

Add tomatoes in an oven-safe dish. Lay fish pieces over the tomatoes; season with seasoning, salt and pepper, and drizzle with melted coconut oil.

Add a cup of water in your Instant Pot and add a trivet.

Place the dish in the pot and lock lid; cook on "Manual" for 5 minutes and then let the pressure come down on its own. Serve along with peeled avocado on the side and season with olive oil.

Creamy Chile Shrimp

Serves: 3 / Prep Time: 5 minutes / Cook Time: 20 minutes

Per Serving: Calories 555; Total Fat 45.0g; Saturated Fat 0.0g; Protein 33.0g; Total Carbs 7.0g; Net Carbs 6.7g; Fiber 0.3g; Sugar 0.0g

Ingredients:
- 1 lb. shrimp
- 1 chile pepper, cut into thin strips

- ½ cup bell pepper, cut into thin strips
- ½ cup white cabbage
- ½ tsp. cayenne powder
- ½ cup chicken stock
- ½ tsp. black pepper
- ½ cup heavy cream
- ½ tsp. hot sauce
- 1 tbsp. garlic, minced
- ½ tsp. lime juice
- ¼ cup canola oil

Directions

Deseed and cut the green chile into thin strips lengthwise.

In the Instant Pot, sauté the bell pepper, cabbage and green chili with half oil for 3-4 minutes. Remove and keep warm by covering with foil.

Sauté ginger and garlic in the Instant Pot with the rest of the oil and add shrimp. Turn off "Sauté" function. Add the spices, hot sauce, and lime juice.

Add chicken stock and cook on high pressure for 4 minutes. Quick pressure release, add the sautéed vegetables and mix well.

Add cream and sauté until the sauce thickens slightly. Serve.

Lemon Kalamata Olive Salmon

Serves: 3 / Prep Time: 10 minutes / Cook Time: 20 minutes

Per Serving: Calories 440; Total Fat 34.0g; Saturated Fat 0.0g; Protein 30.0g; Total Carbs 3.0g; Net Carbs 3.0g; Fiber 0.0g; Sugar 0.0g

Ingredients:
- 4 x 0.3 lb. salmon filets
- 2 tbsps. fresh lemon juice

- ¼ tsp. black pepper
- ½ cup red onion, sliced
- 1 tsp. herbs de Provence
- 1 can pitted kalamata olives
- 1tsp. sea salt
- ½ lemon, thinly sliced
- 1 cup fish broth
- ½ tsp. cumin
- ½ cup olive oil

Directions

Generously season salmon fillets with cumin, pepper, and salt; set your Instant Pot on "Sauté" mode and heat the olive oil; add fish and brown both sides.

Stir the remaining ingredients into the pot and bring to a simmer; lock lid. Set your pot on manual high for 10 minutes; when done, quick release pressure and then serve.

Seafood Medley Stew

Serves: 3 / Prep Time: 5 minutes / Cook Time: 20 minutes

Per Serving: Calories 535; Total Fat 44.0g; Saturated Fat 0.0g; Protein 27.0g; Total Carbs 8.0g; Net Carbs 7.6g; Fiber 0.4g; Sugar 0.0g

Ingredients:
- 2 cups chicken broth
- 2 tbsps. lemon juice
- ½ lb. shrimp
- ½ lb. mussels

- 2 cloves garlic, crushed
- ½ cup coconut cream
- ½ tsp. black pepper
- 100 g. halibut
- 1 dried whole star anise
- 1 bay leaf
- 1 cup light cream
- 3 tbsps. coconut oil

Directions

In the Instant Pot, sauté the bay leaves, and star anise in coconut oil for about 30 seconds.

Add garlic and continue to sauté.

Add broth. Rub lemon juice, salt, and pepper on fish fillets and place in the pot. Add shrimp and mussels as well.

Cook for 10 minutes. Release pressure naturally.

Add the two creams and allow to simmer.

Remove bay leaves and star anise before serving.

Flavored Octopus

Serves: 4 / Prep Time: 10 minutes / Cook Time: 8 minutes

Per Serving: Calories 120; Total Fat 3.0g; Saturated Fat 0.0g; Protein 30.0g; Total Carbs 1.5g; Net Carbs 1.5g; Fiber 0.0g; Sugar 0.0g

Ingredients:
- 1 tsp chopped cilantro
- 2 tbsps. olive oil
- 0.6 pounds octopus
- 2 tsps. garlic powder

- 3 tbsps. lime juice
- salt and pepper, to taste

Directions

Place the octopus in the steaming basket. Season with garlic powder, salt, and pepper. Drizzle with olive and lime juice.

Pour the water into the Instant Pot and lower the steaming basket. Close the lid and cook for 8 minutes on high.

Do a quick pressure release.

Serve and enjoy!

Caramelized Tilapia

Serves: 4 / Prep Time: 30 minutes / Cook Time: 20 minutes

Per Serving: Calories 150; Total Fat 4.0g; Saturated Fat 0.0g; Protein 21.0g; Total Carbs 3.0g; Net Carbs 2.4g; Fiber 0.6g; Sugar 0.0g

Ingredients:
- 1-pound tilapia fillets
- 1 red chili, minced
- 3 tsp. minced garlic
- ¼ cup granulated sweetener
- 1 spring onion, minced

- ¾ cup coconut water
- 1/3 cup water
- 3 tbsp. fish sauce
- salt and pepper, to taste

Directions:

In a bowl, combine the fish sauce, garlic, salt, and pepper. Place the tilapia inside and mix to coat. Cover and let sit in the fridge for 30 minutes.

Meanwhile, combine the water and sweetener in the Instant Pot. Cook on "Sauté" until caramelized.

Add fish and pour the coconut water over. Close the lid and cook on high for 10 minutes.

Do a quick pressure release. Top the fish with spring onion and chili.

Serve and enjoy!

Crunchy Almond Tuna

Serves: 4 / Prep Time: 5 minutes / Cook Time: 3 minutes

Per Serving: Calories 150; Total Fat 5.0g; Saturated Fat 0.0g; Protein 10.0g; Total Carbs 4.0g; Net Carbs 4.0g; Fiber 0.0g; Sugar 0.0g

Ingredients:
- 2 cans of tuna, drained
- 1 cup shaved almond
- 2 tbsps. butter

- 1 tsp garlic powder
- 1 cup grated cheddar cheese

Directions

Melt the butter in your Instant Pot on "Sauté." Add tuna, almonds, garlic powder, and cheddar. Cook on "Sauté" for 3 minutes.

Serve immediately over cauliflower, rice or on its own.

Side Dishes and Vegetables

Veggie Scramble

Serves: 4 / Prep Time: 10 minutes / Cook Time: 20 minutes

Per Serving: Calories 203; Total Fat 5.0g; Saturated Fat 0.0g; Protein 20.0g; Total Carbs 12.0g; Net Carbs 9.0g; Fiber 3.0g; Sugar 5.0g

Ingredients:
- 4 egg whites
- 1 egg yolk
- 2 tbsps. almond milk

- 1 cup spinach
- 1 tomato, chopped
- ½ white onion, chopped
- 3 fresh basil leaves, chopped
- salt and pepper, to taste
- ghee

Directions

In a bowl, whisk the egg yolk and whites with the milk. Stir well.

Heat the ghee in a pan over medium heat. Add the onions and sauté until fragrant.

Add in the tomato to the pan with the spinach and cook until the spinach is almost wilted.

Pour the egg mixture over the spinach and cook until firm (or until the egg sets). Stir constantly. Season with salt and pepper.

Serve warm!

Egg Loaf

Serves: 6 / Prep Time: 5 minutes / Cook Time: 4 minutes

Per Serving: Calories 74; Total Fat 5.0g; Saturated Fat 1.0g; Protein 6.0g; Total Carbs 0.3g; Net Carbs 0.3g; Fiber 0.0g; Sugar 0.0g

Ingredients:
- unsalted butter, for greasing the bowl
- 6 eggs

- 2 cups water, for steaming

Directions

Grease a heatproof bowl with the butter extremely well.

Crack the eggs into the greased bowl, keeping the yolks intact. Cover the bowl with aluminum foil and set aside briefly.

Pour the water into the inner cooking pot and place a trivet on top. Place the foil-covered bowl of eggs on the trivet.

Close the lid, Select "Pressure Cook" or "Manual," and adjust the pressure to high and cook for 4 minutes. Quick-release the pressure when the cooking is complete.

Carefully remove the bowl from the pot. Pop out the egg loaf from the bowl. You'll see mainly a loaf of egg white, with just a few spots of egg yolk.

Chop the egg loaf as coarse or fine as you'd like. You can now mix it with a little mayonnaise for egg salad, stir it with a little butter, salt, and pepper for a quick snack or meal.

Asparagus with Colby Cheese

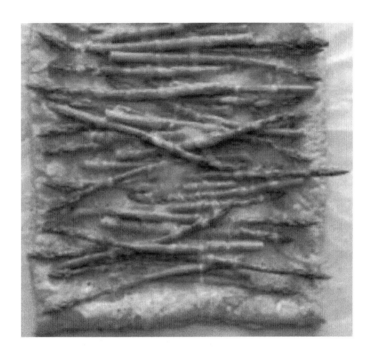

Serves: 4 / Prep Time: 5 minutes / Cook Time: 5 minutes

Per Serving: Calories 164; Total Fat 12.2g; Saturated Fat 3.1g; Protein 7.8g; Total Carbs 8.7g; Net Carbs 8.1g; Fiber 0.6g; Sugar 3.3g

Ingredients:
- 1 ½ pounds fresh asparagus
- 2 tablespoons olive oil
- 4 garlic cloves, minced

- sea salt, to taste
- ¼ teaspoon ground black pepper
- ½ cup Colby cheese, shredded

Directions

Add 1 cup of water and a steamer basket to your Instant Pot.

Now, place the asparagus on the steamer basket; drizzle your asparagus with olive oil. Scatter garlic over the top of the asparagus. Season with salt and black pepper.

Secure the lid. Choose "Manual" mode and high pressure; cook for 1 minute. Once cooking is complete, use a quick pressure release; carefully remove the lid.

Transfer the prepared asparagus to a nice serving platter and scatter shredded cheese over the top. Enjoy!

Mexican-Style Zucchini and Poblanos

Serves: 6 / Prep Time: 5 minutes / Cook Time: 10 minutes

Per Serving: Calories 248; Total Fat 20.0g; Saturated Fat 4.1g; Protein 14.0g; Total Carbs 3.0g; Net Carbs 2.0g; Fiber 1.0g; Sugar 1.0g

Ingredients:
- 1 tablespoon vegetable oil
- 2 poblano peppers, seeded and cut lengthwise into ½-inch strips
- 2 teaspoons unsalted butter

- ½ onion, thinly sliced
- 1 tablespoon minced garlic
- 1-pound ground pork
- 1 zucchini, cut into thick rounds
- 1 yellow crookneck squash, cut into thick rounds
- ½ cup chicken broth
- ½ teaspoon ground cumin
- 1 teaspoon salt
- 1 tablespoon Mexican crema or sour cream

Directions

Select "Sauté" to preheat the Instant Pot and adjust to high heat. When the hot, add the oil and allow it to shimmer. Add the poblano strips in a single layer, working in batches if necessary, and char on both sides, flipping only occasionally, for about 10 minutes.

Add the butter to the pot. Once melted, add the onion and garlic, and sauté until soft, 2 to 3 minutes.

Add the ground pork and break it into chunks, mixing it well with the vegetables. Cook until the lumps are broken up in the meat, and it is half-way cooked, about 4 to 5 minutes.

Add the zucchini, squash, broth, cumin, and salt to the pot.

Lock the lid. Select "Pressure Cook" or "Manual" and set pressure to low. Cook for 2 minutes. When the cooking is complete, quick-release the pressure. Unlock the lid.

Stir in the cream, so it fully incorporates into the sauce.

Vegetables à la Grecque

Serves: 4 / Prep Time: 6 minutes / Cook Time: 8 minutes

Per Serving: Calories 326; Total Fat 25.1g; Saturated Fat 0.0g; Protein 15.7g; Total Carbs 8.4g; Net Carbs 6.4g; Fiber 2.0g; Sugar 4.3g

Ingredients:
- 2 tablespoons olive oil
- 2 garlic cloves, minced
- 1 red onion, chopped
- 0.6 pounds button mushrooms, thinly sliced

- 1 eggplant, sliced
- ½ teaspoon dried basil
- 1 teaspoon dried oregano
- 1 thyme sprig, leaves picked
- 2 rosemary sprigs, leaves picked
- ½ cup tomato sauce
- ¼ cup dry Greek wine
- ¼ cup water
- 0.5 pounds Halloumi cheese, cubed
- 4 tablespoons Kalamata olives, pitted and halved

Directions

Press the "Sauté" button to heat up your Instant Pot; now, heat the olive oil. Cook the garlic and red onions for 1 to 2 minutes, stirring periodically.

Stir in the mushrooms and continue to sauté an additional 2 to 3 minutes.

Add the eggplant, basil, oregano, thyme, rosemary, tomato sauce, Greek wine, and water.

Secure the lid. Choose "Manual" mode and low pressure; cook for 3 minutes. Once cooking is complete, use a quick pressure release; carefully remove the lid.

Top with cheese and olives.

Simple Basil Pesto Zucchini

Serves: 4 / Prep Time: 10 minutes / Cook Time: 5 minutes

Per Serving: Calories 214; Total Fat 17.4g; Saturated Fat 0.0g; Protein 5.0g; Total Carbs 7.9g; Net Carbs 2.2g; Fiber 5.7g; Sugar 0.0g

Ingredients:
- 1 cup mozzarella cheese
- 1 large red bell pepper, cut into strips
- 2 medium-sized zucchinis, thinly sliced
- 2 tbsps. olive oil

- 1 medium-sized eggplant, thinly sliced
- 1 tsp. Italian seasoning
- 1 cup vegetable stock

For the basil pesto:

- ½ tsp garlic powder
- 2 tsps. balsamic vinegar
- ½ tsp. black pepper, freshly ground
- 2 tbsps. fresh basil, finely chopped
- 2 tbsps. sour cream
- 3 tbsps. olive oil
- ¼ tsp. mustard seeds

Directions

Combine sliced zucchinis, stripped red bell pepper, and sliced eggplant in a large bowl. Drizzle with olive oil and Italian seasoning. Optionally, add a pinch of salt and mix well with your hands. Set aside.

Combine all pesto ingredients in a food processor and blend until smooth and creamy. Then set aside.

Plug in the Instant Pot add vegetables in the stainless steel insert. Pour in the vegetable stock and close the lid. Adjust the steam release handle and press the "Manual" button. Set the timer for 8 minutes and cook on high pressure.

When done; perform a quick pressure release by moving the valve to the "Venting" position.

Open the pot and transfer the vegetables to a serving plate. Top with basil pesto and serve immediately.

Optionally, garnish with some fresh basil leaves and enjoy!

Celery Spinach Stew

Serves: 4 / Prep Time: 3 minutes / Cook Time: 12 minutes

Per Serving: Calories 278; Total Fat 28.2g; Saturated Fat 1.0g; Protein 2.3g; Total Carbs 4.6g; Net Carbs 3.2g; Fiber 1.4g; Sugar 0.0g

Ingredients:
- 2 cups fresh spinach, chopped
- 1 small onion, chopped
- 1 cup celery leaves, chopped

- 2 cups heavy cream
- 1 tbsp. lemon juice
- 2 tbsps. butter
- 1 cup celery stalks, chopped
- 2 garlic cloves, minced
- 1/2 tsp. black pepper, ground
- 1 tbsp. fresh mint, torn
- 1 tsp. salt

Directions

In a large colander, combine spinach and celery. Rinse well under running water and drain. Transfer to a cutting board cut into bite-sized pieces. Set aside.

Plug in your instant pot and press the "Sauté" button. Add butter and stir constantly until melts.

Add celery stalks, garlic, and onions. Cook for 2 minutes and add celery leaves and spinach. Sprinkle with salt and pepper. Cook for 2 - 3 minutes and pour in the heavy cream.

Securely lock the lid and press the "Manual" button. Adjust the steam release handle and set the timer for 5 minutes. Cook on high pressure.

When you hear the cooker's end signal, perform a quick release of the pressure and open the pot.

Stir in the mint and lemon juice. Let it chill for 5 minutes before serving.

Tasty Creamy Collard Greens

Serves: 4 / Prep Time: 10 minutes / Cook Time: 15 minutes

Per Serving: Calories 214; Total Fat 17.6g; Saturated Fat 1.0g; Protein 5.7g; Total Carbs 24.6g; Net Carbs 7.7g; Fiber 17.6g; Sugar 0.0g

Ingredients:
- 1 lb. collard greens, chopped
- 1 medium-sized onion, chopped
- ½ cup bacon, cut into bite-sized pieces
- 2 garlic cloves, finely chopped
- 1 cup sour cream

- ½ tsp. balsamic vinegar
- 1 tbsp. olive oil
- ¼ tsp. black pepper, ground
- ½ tsp. Italian seasoning
- 1 tsp. red pepper flakes
- 1 tsp. sea salt

Directions

Plug in your Instant Pot and add the bacon to the stainless-steel insert. Press the "Sauté" button and cook for 3 - 4 minutes, or until crisp. Remove the bacon from the pot and add olive oil. When hot, add onions and garlic. Stir-fry for 3 - 4 minutes, or until the onions translucent.

Add collard greens and cook for 2 minutes. Sprinkle with salt, pepper, Italian seasoning, and red pepper flakes. Pour in 1 cup of water and securely lock the lid. Adjust the steam release handle and press the "Manual" button. Set the timer for 5 minutes and cook on high pressure.

When done, perform a quick pressure release and open the pot.

Stir in the sour cream, balsamic vinegar, and bacon. Press the "Sauté" button and cook for 2 - 3 minutes more, or until heated through. Turn off the pot and transfer all to a serving plate.

Onion Cauliflower Hash

Serves: 3 / Prep Time: 7 minutes / Cook Time: 13 minutes

Per Serving: Calories 217; Total Fat 13.7g; Saturated Fat 0.1g; Protein 10.3g; Total Carbs 11.3g; Net Carbs 5.0g; Fiber 6.3g; Sugar 0.0g

Ingredients:
- 1 lb. cauliflower, chopped
- 1 cup green cabbage, shredded
- 2 medium-sized onions, sliced
- ¼ cup parmesan cheese
- 1 cup vegetable stock

- 2 tbsps. olive oil
- ¼ tsp. black pepper, ground
- ½ tsp. dried thyme, ground
- ½ tsp. smoked paprika, ground
- 1 tsp. salt

Directions

Plug in the Instant Pot and grease the stainless steel insert with olive oil. Press the "Sauté" button and add cauliflower and onions. Sprinkle with salt, pepper, and thyme. Stir well and cook for 5 minutes.

Add cabbage and pour in the vegetables stock. Stir again and securely lock the lid. Set the steam release handle and press the "Manual" button. Set the timer for 8 minutes and cook on high pressure.

When you hear the cooker's end signal, perform a quick release of the pressure by moving the valve to the "Venting" position. Open the pot and stir in the thyme and smoked paprika.

Transfer all to a serving plate and sprinkle with parmesan cheese before serving.

Steamed Broccoli with Basil

Serves: 3 / Prep Time: 10 minutes / Cook Time: 10 minutes

Per Serving: Calories 187; Total Fat 10.8g; Saturated Fat 0.0g; Protein 10.4g; Total Carbs 10.0g; Net Carbs 4.0g; Fiber 6.0g; Sugar 0.0g

Ingredients:
- 1 lb. broccoli, chopped
- 2 garlic cloves, peeled
- ½ cup fresh basil, chopped
- ½ cup cottage cheese
- ½ cup avocado, chopped
- 1 tbsp. olive oil

- 1 tbsp. lemon juice, freshly squeezed
- ¼ tsp. dried oregano, ground
- ½ tsp. red pepper, ground
- ¼ tsp. dried parsley, ground
- 1 tsp. salt

Directions

Plug in the Instant Pot and pour in 1 cup of water in the stainless steel insert.

Place the trivet on the bottom of the pot and set the steam basket on top. Place broccoli in the steam basket and sprinkle with salt and pepper. Close the lid and set the steam release handle by moving the valve to the "Sealing" position. Press the "Steam" button and set the timer for 10 minutes.

Meanwhile, combine basil, cottage cheese, avocado, garlic, olive oil, lemon juice, red pepper, parsley, and oregano in a food processor. Pulse until smooth and totally incorporated.

When you hear the cooker's end signal, release the pressure naturally. Open the pot and transfer the broccoli to a serving plate. Top with basil cream and serve immediately!

Sautéed Vegetables

Serves: 3 / Prep Time: 5 minutes / Cook Time: 10 minutes

Per Serving: Calories 171; Total Fat 12.0g; Saturated Fat 0.0g; Protein 5.3g; Total Carbs 9.3g; Net Carbs 4.5g; Fiber 4.8g; Sugar 0.0g

Ingredients:
- 1 red bell pepper, sliced
- 1 small onion, sliced

- 1 small zucchini, cut into cubes
- 1 green bell pepper, sliced
- ¼ cup dried porcini mushrooms
- ¼ cup Feta cheese
- ½ cup sour cream
- 2 tbsps. tamari sauce
- 2 tbsps. sesame oil
- ½ tsp. dried thyme
- ¼ tsp. dried oregano
- 1 tsp. pink Himalayan salt

Directions

Plug in the instant pot and press the "Sauté" button. Heat up the sesame oil and add zucchini. Sprinkle with some salt and cook for 5 - 6 minutes, stirring constantly.

Now add bell peppers and onions. Sprinkle with tamari sauce and give it a good stir. Optionally, drizzle with some rice vinegar.

Season with some more salt, thyme, and oregano. Continue to cook for 2 - 3 minutes and then add Feta cheese and mushrooms. Pour in about three tablespoons of water and cook for 3 - 4 minutes.

When done, press the "Cancel" button and stir in the sour cream. To enjoy, serve it immediately.

Stuffed Bell Peppers

Serves: 3 / Prep Time: 8 minutes / Cook Time: 30 minutes

Per Serving: Calories 202; Total Fat 16.0g; Saturated Fat 0.0g; Protein 8.3g; Total Carbs 7.1g; Net Carbs 5.4g; Fiber 1.7g; Sugar 0.0g

Ingredients:
- 2 medium-sized yellow bell peppers, halved
- ½ cup mozzarella cheese
- ½ cup tomatoes, diced
- 2 medium-sized green bell pepper, halved

- 2 cups button mushrooms, diced
- 1 cup feta cheese, crumbled
- 2 tbsps. celery leaves, finely chopped
- 2 tbsps. olive oil
- ½ tsp. black pepper, ground
- ½ tsp. smoked paprika, ground
- ¼ tsp. cayenne pepper, ground
- ½ tsp. salt

Directions

Cut the bell peppers in half and remove the stem and seeds. Set aside.

In a large mixing bowl, combine button mushrooms, feta cheese, mozzarella cheese, tomatoes, celery, and olive oil. Add all spices and mix until well incorporated. Stuff the bell pepper halves with this mixture. Use some additional oil to brush the peppers from outside.

Line some parchment paper over a fitting springform pan and set aside

Plug in the instant pot and pour 1 cup of water in the stainless steel insert. Set the trivet on the bottom and place the stuffed peppers on top.

Close the lid and set the steam release handle. Press the "Manual" button and set the timer for 30 minutes. Cook on high pressure.

When done, perform a quick pressure release and open the pot.

Transfer the peppers to a serving plate and sprinkle with some dried oregano or dried rosemary before serving. Optionally, top with Greek yogurt.

Desserts and Smoothies

Pumpkin Pie Pudding

Serves: 6 / Prep Time: 10 minutes / Cook Time: 20 minutes

Per Serving: Calories 188; Total Fat 17.0g; Saturated Fat 0.0g; Protein 4.0g; Total Carbs 8.0g; Net Carbs 6.0g; Fiber 2.0g; Sugar 3.0g

Ingredients:
- nonstick cooking spray
- 2 eggs

- ½ cup heavy (whipping) cream or almond milk
- ¾ cup Swerve
- 1 pound can pumpkin purée
- 1 teaspoon pumpkin pie spice
- 1 teaspoon vanilla extract

For finishing:
- ½ cup heavy (whipping) cream

Directions

Grease a pan well with the cooking spray, making sure it gets into all the crannies and nooks.

In a medium bowl, whisk the eggs. Add the cream, Swerve, pumpkin purée, pumpkin pie spice, and vanilla, and stir to mix thoroughly.

Transfer the mixture into the pan and use aluminum foil or silicone lid cover it.

Pour water (2 cups) into the inner cooking pot, and then put a trivet in the pot. Put the pan on the trivet.

Latch the lid. Select "Pressure Cook" or "Manual" and set pressure to high and cook for 20 minutes. After the time finishes, allow 10 minutes to naturally release the pressure. For any remaining pressure, just quick-release it. Open the lid.

Remove the pan and place it in the refrigerator. Chill for about 7 hours.

When ready to serve, finish by making the whipped cream. Using a hand mixer, beat the heavy cream until it forms soft peaks. Do not overbeat and turn it to butter. Serve each pudding with a dollop of whipped cream.

Keto Celery and Nut Smoothie

Serves: 6 / Prep Time: 10 minutes / Cook Time: 30 minutes

Per Serving: Calories 220; Total Fat 14.0g; Saturated Fat 0.0g; Protein 5.0g; Total Carbs 9.0g; Net Carbs 7.0g; Fiber 2.0g; Sugar 1.0g

Ingredients:
- 2 celery stems
- 1 cup spinach leaves, roughly chopped

- ½ cup unsalted pistachio nuts
- ½ avocado, chopped
- ½ cup lime, juice
- 1 tbsp. Hemp seeds
- 1 tbsp. almonds, soaked
- 1 cup coconut water
- ice cubes (optional)

Directions

Add all ingredients in a blender with a few ice cubes and blend until smooth.

Serve and enjoy!

Coconut-Almond Cake

Serves: 8 / Prep Time: 10 minutes / Cook Time: 40 minutes

Per Serving: Calories 231; Total Fat 19.0g; Saturated Fat 0.4g; Protein 3.0g; Total Carbs 12.0g; Net Carbs 10.0g; Fiber 2.0g; Sugar 1.0g

Ingredients:
- nonstick cooking spray
- 1 cup almond flour
- ½ cup unsweetened shredded coconut
- ⅓ cup Swerve
- 1 teaspoon apple pie spice

- 2 eggs, lightly whisked
- ¼ cup unsalted butter, melted
- ½ cup heavy (whipping) cream

Directions

Grease a 6-inch round cake pan with the cooking spray.

In a medium bowl, mix together the almond flour, coconut, Swerve, and apple pie spice. Add the eggs, then the butter, and then the cream, mixing well after each addition.

Pour the batter into the pan and cover with aluminum foil. Pour 2 cups of water into the inner cooking pot, then place a trivet in the pot. Place the pan on the trivet.

Latch the lid. Select "Pressure Cook" or "Manual" and set pressure to high and cook for 40 minutes. After the time finishes, allow 10 minutes to naturally release the pressure. For any remaining pressure, just quick-release it. Open the lid.

Carefully take out the pan and let it cool for 15 to 20 minutes. Invert the cake onto a plate. Sprinkle with shredded coconut, almond slices, or powdered sweetener, if desired, and serve.

Dark Chocolate Cake

Serves: 6 / Prep Time: 10 minutes / Cook Time: 20 minutes

Per Serving: Calories 225; Total Fat 20.0g; Saturated Fat 0.0g; Protein 5.0g; Total Carbs 4.0g; Net Carbs 2.0g; Fiber 2.0g; Sugar 0.0g

Ingredients:
- 1 cup almond flour
- ⅔ cup Swerve
- ¼ cup unsweetened cocoa powder
- ¼ cup chopped walnuts

- 1 teaspoon baking powder
- 3 eggs
- ⅓ cup heavy (whipping) cream
- ¼ cup coconut oil
- nonstick cooking spray

Directions

Put the flour, Swerve, cocoa powder, walnuts, baking powder, eggs, cream, and coconut oil in a large bowl. Using a hand mixer on high speed, combine the ingredients until the mixture is well incorporated and looks fluffy. This step will keep the cake from being too dense.

With the cooking spray, grease a heatproof pan, such as a 3-cup Bundt pan, that fits inside your Instant Pot. Pour the cake batter into the pan and cover with aluminum foil.

Pour 2 cups of water into the inner cooking pot, then place a trivet in the pot. Place the pan on the trivet.

Latch the lid. Select "Pressure Cook" or "Manual" and set pressure to high and cook for 20 minutes. After the time finishes, allow 10 minutes to naturally release the pressure. For any remaining pressure, just quick-release it. Carefully remove the pan and let it cool for 15 to 20 minutes. Invert the cake onto a plate. It can be served hot or at room temperature. Serve with a dollop of whipped cream, if desired.

Vanilla Cream with Raspberries

Serves: 4 / Prep Time: 10 minutes / Cook Time: 40 minutes

Per Serving: Calories 302; Total Fat 30.7g; Saturated Fat 1.0g; Protein 4.2g; Total Carbs 4.0g; Net Carbs 1.3g; Fiber 2.7g; Sugar 1.8g

Ingredients:
- 1 ½ cup coconut milk, full-fat
- 1 tbsp. almond flour
- 2 tbsps. butter
- ¼ cup raspberries
- 3 egg yolks
- 3 tbsps. Swerve

- 1 tbsp. agar powder
- 1 vanilla bean
- 2 tsps. vanilla extract

Directions

Using a sharp paring knife, slice the vanilla bean lengthwise and remove the seeds, set aside.

Plug in the instant pot and press the "Sauté" button.

Grease the inner pot with butter and add coconut milk. Warm up, stirring constantly, and then add egg yolks, swerve, and vanilla extract.

Cook for 3 - 4 minutes, stirring constantly.

Finally, add agar powder, and vanilla seeds. Give it a good stir and continue to cook for another couple of minutes, or until the mixture thickens.

Press the "Cancel" button and remove the cream from the pot. Divide between serving bowls and optionally top with some whipped cream or fresh strawberries.

Plug in the instant pot and pour in the milk. Press the "Sauté" button and heat up. Add Swerve, cocoa powder, coconut cream, and vanilla extract.

Bring it to a boil, stirring constantly, and then add agar powder. Continue to cook for 1 - 2 minutes.

Press the "Cancel" button and stir in finely chopped almonds.

Transfer the mixture to a large mixing bowl and pour in the whipping cream. Beat well on high speed for 2 - 3 minutes.

Finally, divide the mixture between serving bowls and top each with raspberries. Serve cold.

Blueberry Almond Smoothie

Serves: 2 / Prep Time: 8 minutes

Per Serving: Calories 314; Total Fat 23.7g; Saturated Fat 0.0g; Protein 16.4g; Total Carbs 8.9g; Net Carbs 8.4g; Fiber 0.5g; Sugar 0.0g

Ingredients:
- 1 lb. almond milk, unsweetened
- 1 tsp. xylitol
- 0.25lb heavy cream

- ¼ cup frozen unsweetened blueberries
- 1 scoop whey vanilla protein

Directions

Place all ingredients in a blender and whip until smooth. Add a little water, if it becomes too thick.

Choco-Cashew Orange Smoothie

Serves: 1 / Prep Time: 7 minutes

Per Serving: Calories 45; Total Fat 1.5g; Saturated Fat 0.0g; Protein 3.0g; Total Carbs 5.7g; Net Carbs 4.7g; Fiber 1.3g; Sugar 0.0g

Ingredients:
- 1 cup cashew milk
- 1 handful of arugula leaves
- 1 tbsp. chocolate whey protein powder

- 1/8 tsp. orange extract

Directions

Place all ingredients in your blender and whip until well combined and smooth.

Add extra ice and serve.

Strawberry Marjoram Smoothie

Serves: 1 / Prep Time: 8 minutes

Per Serving: Calories 292; Total Fat 26.7g; Saturated Fat 0.6g; Protein 2.8g; Total Carbs 6.2g; Net Carbs 5.4g; Fiber 0.8g; Sugar 0.3g

Ingredients:

- ¼ cup fresh or frozen strawberries
- 2 fresh marjoram leaves
- 2 tbsps. heavy cream

- 1 cup unsweetened coconut milk
- 1 tbsp. sugar-free vanilla syrup
- ½ tsp. pure vanilla extract
- ice cubes

Directions

Place all ingredients in your blender and mix until it becomes smooth. If you wish, you can add the ice cubes. Serve and enjoy!

Keto Avocado Smoothie

Serves: 3 / Prep Time: 7 minutes

Per Serving: Calories 252; Total Fat 24.4g; Saturated Fat 0.0g; Protein 3.7g; Total Carbs 8.4g; Net Carbs 2.9g; Fiber 5.5g; Sugar 0.0g

Ingredients:
- 1 avocado
- 0.2 lb. almond milk, unsweetened
- 0.2 lb. heavy whipping cream
- 6 drops Liquid Stevia
- ice cubes

Directions

Cut the avocado in half, remove the seed, and remove the flesh from the skin.

In a blender, mix the almond milk, avocado, heavy whipping cream, sweetener and ice cubes. Blend 1 minute.

Serve and enjoy!

Raspberry and Spinach Smoothie

Serves: 1 / Prep Time: 5 minutes

Per Serving: Calories 450; Total Fat 34.0g; Saturated Fat 1.0g; Protein 35.0g; Total Carbs 6.0g; Net Carbs 0.6g; Fiber 5.4g; Sugar 2.1g

Ingredients:
- 4 walnuts
- 4 raspberries
- 1 cup spinach

- 1 tsp. protein powder
- 2 tbsps. heavy cream
- 1 tsp. chia seeds
- 1 tbsp. coconut oil
- ½ cup almond milk
- ice cubes

Directions

Pour the liquid ingredients into your blender (starting with the liquid will protect your blades).

Add the remaining ingredients. Blend for a couple of minutes, or until it becomes smooth.

Serve and enjoy!

Caramel Coffee Smoothie

Serves: 4 / Prep Time: 5 minutes

Per Serving: Calories 171; Total Fat 15.0g; Saturated Fat 2.0g; Protein 2.8g; Total Carbs 9.1g; Net Carbs 7.1g; Fiber 2.0g; Sugar 0.0g

Ingredients:
- ½ cup heavy cream
- ½ cup almond milk, unsweetened
- 3 tbsps. sugar-free chocolate syrup

- 3 tbsps. sugar-free caramel syrup
- ¾ cup cold coffee
- 2 tbsps. cocoa, unsweetened
- ice cubes

Directions

In a blender, add all ingredients and blend until incorporated well.

Pour into glasses and serve.

Almond Choc Shake

Serves: 2 / Prep Time: 5 minutes

Per Serving: Calories 292; Total Fat 25.0g; Saturated Fat 0.0g; Protein 15.3g; Total Carbs 4.4g; Net Carbs 2.4g; Fiber 2.0g; Sugar 0.0g

Ingredients:
- 1 lb. almond milk, unsweetened
- 1 tbsp. chia seeds
- 1 tsp. xylitol

- ½ tsp cacao powder
- 0.25 lb. heavy cream
- 2 tbs. scoop Whey Chocolate Isolate powder
- ½ cup crushed ice

Directions

Add all ingredients into the blender and whip until smooth.

Serve and enjoy!

Green Coconut Smoothie

Serves: 2 / Prep Time: 10 minutes

Per Serving: Calories 217; Total Fat 16.6g; Saturated Fat 1.0g; Protein 2.9g; Total Carbs 9.0g; Net Carbs 5.0g; Fiber 4.0g; Sugar 0.0g

Ingredients:
- 1 cup coconut milk
- 1 green apple, cored and chopped
- 1 cup spinach

- 1 cucumber
- 2 tbsps. shaved coconut
- 1/2 cup water
- ice cubes (if needed)

Directions

Put all ingredients and ice in a blender; pulse until smooth.

Serve immediately.

Avocado Pudding

Serves: 2 / Prep Time: 5 minutes / Cook Time: 3 minutes

Per Serving: Calories 251; Total Fat 20.9g; Saturated Fat 1.0g; Protein 5.6g; Total Carbs 7.9g; Net Carbs 3.7g; Fiber 4.2g; Sugar 0.0g

Ingredients:

- ½ ripe avocado, cut into cubes
- 1 tsp. agar powder
- 1 cup whole milk

- ¼ cup coconut cream
- 2 tsps. Stevia powder
- 1 tsp. vanilla extract

Directions

Combine avocado and coconut cream in a food processor or a high-speed blender. Pulse until smooth and creamy. Then set aside.

In a large mixing bowl, combine milk, agar powder, Stevia, and vanilla extract. Mix until well combined and then add avocado mixture. Stir all well and pour into an oven-safe bowl.

Pour 1 cup of water in the stainless steel insert of your Instant Pot. Set the trivet on the bottom and place the bowl on top.

Securely lock the lid and set the steam release handle by moving the valve to the "Sealing" position. Set the timer for 3 minutes on the "Manual" mode.

When you hear the cooker's end signal, perform a quick pressure release and open the pot.

Transfer the bowl to a wire rack and let it cool completely.

Refrigerate for 30 minutes before serving. Enjoy!

Conclusion

Thanks for taking a culinary adventure in this book. Let's hope you now have all of the essential tools to achieve your goals.

The next step is to start working on developing a healthier lifestyle by incorporating this ketogenic diet using the Instant Pot into your lifestyle. In order to get healthy, you must make changes to how we see food. Food is not the enemy: it is meant to nourish us and provide the nutrients you need to sustain a viable life. Without eating properly, we develop disease and illness, as well as, excess fat. By using the keto diet, you can start to change the way you eat and process your foods and make healthy lifestyle choices that will have a positive impact on the rest of our lives.

The ketogenic diet will help you achieve your health goals, but just like any other diets, your commitment and perseverance to follow this diet are needed for you to reap its benefits. Use the tips, recipes, and meal plans that I shared with you during the first weeks of your keto diet. Also, don't be afraid to explore other recipes that you wish to include in your meal plan. As long as you stay within the numbers of the required macros, you need to consume, then you're assured that your body will continuously burn fat.

Try the ketogenic diet and gain mental clarity, burn excess fat, and have unlimited energy starting today!

Conversion Tables

VOLUME EQUIVALENTS (LIQUID)

US STANDARD	US STANDARD (OUNCES)	METRIC (APPROXIMATE)
2 tablespoons	1 fl. oz.	30 mL
¼ cup	2 fl. oz.	60 mL
½ cup	4 fl. oz.	120 mL
1 cup	8 fl. oz.	240 mL
1½ cups	12 fl. oz.	355 mL
2 cups or 1 pint	16 fl. oz.	475 mL
4 cups or 1 quart	32 fl. oz.	1 L
1 gallon	128 fl. oz.	4 L

VOLUME EQUIVALENTS (DRY)

US STANDARD	METRIC (APPROXIMATE)
⅛ teaspoon	0.5 mL
¼ teaspoon	1 mL
½ teaspoon	2 mL
¾ teaspoon	4 mL
1 teaspoon	5 mL
1 tablespoon	15 mL
¼ cup	59 mL
⅓ cup	79 mL
½ cup	118 mL
⅔ cup	156 mL
¾ cup	177 mL
1 cup	235 mL
2 cups or 1 pint	475 mL
3 cups	700 mL
4 cups or 1 quart	1 L

TEMPERATURES

FAHRENHEIT (F)	CELSIUS (C) (APPROXIMATE)
250°F	120°C
300°F	150°C
325°F	165°C
350°F	180°C
375°F	190°C
400°F	200°C
425°F	220°C
450°F	230°C

WEIGHT

US STANDARD	METRIC (APPROXIMATE)
½ ounce	15 g
1 ounce	30 g
2 ounces	60 g
4 ounces	115 g
8 ounces	225 g
12 ounces	340 g
16 ounces or 1 pound	455 g

Made in the USA
San Bernardino, CA
01 March 2020